WITHDRAWN FROM
MACALESTER COLLEGE
LIBRARY

D0141903

Essays on the Anthropology of Reason

EDITORS

Sherry B. Ortner, Nicholas B. Dirks, Geoff Eley

A LIST OF TITLES

IN THIS SERIES APPEARS

AT THE BACK OF

THE BOOK

PRINCETON STUDIES IN

CULTURE / POWER / HISTORY

Essays on the Anthropology of Reason

Paul Rabinow

PRINCETON UNIVERSITY PRESS

PRINCETON, NEW JERSEY

Copyright © 1996 by Princeton University Press
Published by Princeton University Press, 41 William Street,
Princeton, New Jersey 08540
In the United Kingdom: Princeton University Press,
Chichester, West Sussex
All Rights Reserved

Library of Congress Cataloging-in-Publication Data

Rabinow, Paul
Essays on the Anthropology of Reason / Paul Rabinow
p.   cm.—(Princeton studies in culture/power/history)
Includes bibliographical references and index.
ISBN 0-691-01159-1 (alk. paper).—
ISBN 0-691-01158-3 (pbk. alk paper)
1. Intellectual life—History—20th century. 2. Science and
civilization. 3. Social sciences—History—20th century.
4. Ethnology—History—20th century. I. Title. II. Series.
CB430.R24   1996
306.4'2—dc20   96-9075

This book has been composed in Baskerville

Princeton University Press books are
printed on acid-free paper and meet the guidelines
for permanence and durability of the Committee
on Production Guidelines for Book Longevity
of the Council on Library Resources

Printed in the United States of America by
Princeton Academic Press

1   2   3   4   5   6   7   8   9   10

1   2   3   4   5   6   7   8   9   10 (pbk.)

IN MEMORY OF

GEORGES CANGUILHEM AND *HANS BLUMENBERG*

Contents

Preface

Invention can be joined to discovery in an art
which is productive of things and arts or skills
rather than of words and arguments or beliefs.
(*Richard McKeon, "The Uses of Rhetoric in a
Technological Age"*)

In order for criticism to be responsible,
it must always be addressed to someone who
can contest it.
(*Talal Asad,* "The Concept of Cultural Translation
in British Social Anthropology")

EACH TEXT in this assemblage was written as an attempt to formulate a problem, to respond to questions, to find a means to move around conceptual, affective, and pragmatic obstacles. Individually and collectively, they articulate working conclusions about specific rationalities and the stance one might adopt toward them. They are forays that helped me to imagine, formulate, reformulate, advance, adapt, and modify a multipronged course of inquiry and reflection. That inquiry was largely about the invention of new techniques, practices, sites, objects, and subjects; it was equally about reflecting on how "new" these things actually were.[1]

Diachronically these essays were researched and written alongside other larger-scale projects. At first I thought of characterizing their place and style as para-ethnographic (*para*, from the Greek, "beside"). However, the more accurate prefix is *dia*.[2] In Greek, *dia* has a range of meaning that is more active and processural than *para*. *Dia* denotes relation and/or motion: throughout (temporal), across, through (something), between or after, through (the instrument or means or manner through which a thing is achieved), mark (a place or space in a line), scatter (spaced intervals). Hence, diachronic, diagrammatic, diagnostic, diasporic, and a term I will return to, dialectic. The texts assembled here are dia-ethnographic, then, in the sense of traversing the ethnos.

But what ethnos? During the early 1980s, I participated in the charged explorations about the nature and legitimacy of ethnographic authority today identified with *Writing Culture*. Then, as now, at the center for me was meeting my own challenge to "anthropologize the West: show how exotic its constitution of reality has been: emphasize those domains most take for granted as universal (this includes epistemology and economics); make them seem as historically peculiar as possible; show how their claims to truth are linked to social practices and have hence become effective forces in the social world."[3] When the agonistic discussion about how to do such things was turned into antagonistic polemic—yet another skirmish in the culture wars—it seemed more fruitful (rather than debating the metaphysics of morals and hypothetical politics) to practice some of the lessons learned.

This frame partially shaped *French Modern*, a book about the genealogy of urban and social planning as a privileged experimental site, where normed forms of modern rationality were turned into a practice and a technocratic politics.[4] I was centrally concerned with the form that modern rationalities were given, one that constituted knowledges in such a manner that they literally obliged the objects (bodies, populations, societies) to be reformed. I sought to understand how a certain type of social actor, "technician of general ideas," emerged, articulated, and experienced the rise and triumph of what Michel Foucault named "biopower." Foucault's definition of bio-power—"what brought life and its mechanisms into the realm of explicit calculations and made knowledge-power an agent of transformation of human life"[5]—was a starting point, a promise of work to come, one Foucault never lived to fulfill. For that reason, substantial parts of *French Modern* were devoted to aspects of the life sciences: to the cholera epidemics in the 1830s, the rise of statistics as a public health tool, the persistence of Lamarckianism in French biology, the political rationality of epidemiology and hygiene.

In the wake of *French Modern*, I began casting about in the emergent cross-over areas (between science, technology, nature, culture, law, politics, and economics) such as the Human Genome Initiative, a mega-project to develop technologies and constituencies in order progressively to map and ultimately reform the genetic makeup of living beings, and the AIDS epidemic with its plague-driven, but not determined, production of new objects, subjectivations, and alliances. Although for contingent reasons I initially veered, or was steered, away from direct work on those topics, they remain key guideposts in our contemporary landscape.

I returned to ethnography, settling on two major participant observation projects in the first five years of the 1990s. The first project was located at Cetus Corporation, a biotechnology company located near Berkeley, California, and later at Roche Molecular Systems in Alameda (see chapter 9). Cetus was the site of invention of the polymerase chain reaction (PCR), an extravagantly flexible technology for the accurate and rapid exponential amplification of precise sequences of DNA. PCR turned genetic scarcity into bounty. It turned genetic bounty into hundreds of millions of dollars. Hundreds of millions of dollars and genetic bounty could be used in many ways, to further many different ends, as in fact has been done. Others outside Cetus have since discovered many different ways to accommodate and elaborate what PCR made possible, and still other contexts have been invented that no one could have imagined without PCR

Although it now appears that PCR was the most important thing to have been produced at Cetus, at the time it was fortuitously in the shadows of projects that management realists and their venture capital backers were certain were far more scientifically and commercially important. Furthermore, PCR was conceived by a highly idiosyncratic individual, Kary Mullis. Mullis, who would have been extremely unlikely to survive at a university or in a pharmaceutical company, was adroitly managed by Tom White, a young scientist given research and development responsibilities he would never have received at that stage of his career in the academic world. These slippages and swerves in status, procedure, and received wisdom highlight specificities of time and place, not some atemporal tale of misrecognized genius. Ultimately, PCR was

a by-product of another invention, an at least momentarily flores-
cent place, located on the volatile 1980s boundaries between the
financial, university, and industrial worlds.[6]

The second fieldwork site was the Centre d'Etude du Polymor-
phisme Humain (CEPH), a genome-mapping center in Paris. The
CEPH is a distinctive institution in France, as it is substantially
funded by public, but not state, moneys, raised by the French dys-
trophy association. It is also known for its technoscientific audac-
ity. Daniel Cohen, then scientific director of the CEPH, keenly
alert that molecular biology and genetics were entering un-
charted ethical and social domains, was eager to establish a "philosophical observatory" at the lab. I was the first experiment. I arrived in late 1993, just after the CEPH had announced the first
(crude) physical map of the human genome, a stunning triumph
over the much better financed American effort. Still exultant, the
CEPH was immediately faced with the quandary, What to do next?
Intense debate and struggle ensued over what scientific goals to
pursue: How does one make abstract scientific goals such as "isolate multifactorial disease genes" into plausible technological
tasks? How does one finance these undertakings in an era when
the nation-state was no longer capable of being the central finan-
cier and regulator of research? Which kind of business and scientific alliances would be the most efficient and the most ethical?
What skills and virtues would such a context demand, and which
ones would it eliminate?

Repeatedly, both in the main projects and in the work that traversed it diagonally, I found myself seeking out "experts" to orient
and instruct me. The content of these intermittent interviews
ranged from a pedagogic presentation of information, to an exposition of concepts, to mild laments or exaltation over everyday
affairs. In this instance, Clifford Geertz's observation that informants' boredom is the anthropologist's best ally did not apply.[7]
Neither the anthropologist nor the informants had much time on
their hands. My interlocutors were busy professionals who gener-
ously afforded me some of their time and knowledge. Their job—
actually their vocation—was to be efficient, accurate, productive,

and inventive. There are few outlets in America's compartmental-
ized and stressed professional culture for practitioners to explain
what they are doing, how they came to do it, and what they think
and feel about doing it. The ethnographic exchange provided
one such opportunity.

Goodwill, or the desire to be recognized, were necessary but not
sufficient to make things happen. As in all such work, there were
any number of other encounters—with people in identical structural positions—that never really "took." When things did click,
there was a supplement, an aroused autocuriosity. This quality was
a dispositional diacritic; some people live that way. The challenge
was to put that reflected curiosity to work. To make it do something. As these professionals were accustomed to making things
work, the challenge for me was to forge research techniques that
would help extend their practice to enrich my own. Existentially,
I found it rewarding ("to take notice of, to recompense") to supplement other forms of ethnographic work with these punctuate,
intensive, face-to-face interactions. Although this technique was
only one among others, it proved salutary in providing a caution
beyond the text and alongside observation, an experimental reality check that at times proved quite surprising, at other times quite
predictable, and, from time to time, quite frustrating—equally appropriate and typical responses to experiments.

These coolly intense interviews were not dialogues in the current sense of the word. More structured than a conversation, these
exchanges obliged both parties to adopt a reflective and refractive
stance toward the situation and themselves. Nor were these exchanges edifying conversations in Richard Rorty's sense; they
were specific, often highly technical—DNA contamination, mito-
chondrial drift, different judicial styles in federal patent courts—
and they did not aim at "moral, intellectual, or spiritual improvement," although, it is true, from time to time some edification
surely resulted. Finally, they were not dialogues in a more philosophic sense either, if by that one means a formal device whereby
seemingly opposed positions are brought to a higher resolution.
There was no resolution because there is and was no underlying
or overarching form toward which we were striving.

Perhaps what was at play was more a kind of dialectic, not in the Hegelian sense of totalities and universal subjects, but more in the Aristotelian sense of an art of invention of topics and common places. One might present the "empty places" that form starting points for specific inquiries, and which are not ends in themselves, as follows. These essays spring from a situated *curiosity*. They take as their domain of inquiry a variety of *emergent* rationalities. They focus especially on scientific *practices*. They proceed from the principle that such practices have some degree of autonomy but conversely that practices must be practiced in *contexts*. They observe that such contexts are often concurrently *invented* to make such practice possible. They argue that practices are *normative*. They conclude that *ethnography* is a practice. This series is assembled post hoc. It could have been "filled in" in different ways. Hence, to represent the contexts in which these essays were written would introduce a kind of retrospective fiction I abjure. Assembling them made them into a new object. However, I note that the first essay generalizes and places in a broader theoretical frame the type of "practice" I have been engaged in, and the last essay reflects on the intellectual and ethical demands of doing the ethnography of science given the present forms of knowledge and types of practitioners.

Today, knowledge-producers are faced with two types of relentless, omnivorous, and insatiable demands. The first demand is to be "effective." In the human sciences, this generally means "operationalizable," good for something else. Although the things produced under this imperative are often imaginary, they can have very real effects, for example, the creation of a prosperous bioethics community. The other demand is for "meaning"; America has a thriving worldview industry. One response to these demands is to accept one or the other, or both. Another is to resist them. I am trying to do neither. Rather, Max Weber's provocation that leading a life of science foregrounds "self-clarification and knowledge of inter-related facts" and "a sense of responsibility" remains, for me, the general demand of the day.[8] However, as one never encounters a general demand, the problem of where to look, how to proceed, and what to do once one gets there is persistently present.

NOTES

1. The idea and occasion for a collection of my work came from Joao Guilherme Biehl, who made the proposal to publish a book of essays in Brazil. We worked together in carrying it out. Joao translated the essays into Portuguese, and in so doing he made punctual, stylistic, and conceptual changes to improve consistency and clarity, many of which we have retained here. While forming the basis for *Antropologia da Razao* (Rio de Janeiro: Relume Dumara, 1996), *Essays in the Anthropology of Reason* contains some different essays and a different progression.

2. James Faubion suggested the use of *dia*. Many thanks to Faubion for this insight and his sustained engagement and support.

3. Paul Rabinow, "Representations Are Social Facts," in J. Clifford and G. Marcus, eds., *Writing Culture: The Poetics and Politics of Ethnography* (Berkeley: University of California Press, 1986), p. 241.

4. *French Modern: Norms and Forms of the Social Environment* (Chicago: University of Chicago Press 1995; orig. MIT Press, 1989).

5. Michel Foucault, *The History of Sexuality*, vol. 1 (New York: Vintage Books, 1980), p. 143.

6. Paul Rabinow, *Making PCR: A Story of Biotechnology* (Chicago: University of Chicago Press, 1996).

7. Clifford Geertz, "Introduction," in *The Interpretation of Cultures* (New York: Basic Books, 1973).

8. Max Weber, "Science as a Vocation," in H. Gerth and C. W. Mills, eds., *From Max Weber* (New York: Oxford University Press, 1946), p. 152.

Acknowledgments

THE FOLLOWING essays have been previously published in slightly different form:

Chapter 2, "Representations Are Social Facts," in *Writing Culture: The Poetics and Politics of Ethnography*, ed. James Clifford and George Marcus (University of California Press, 1986). Chapter 3, "On the Archaeology of Late Modernity," published as "France in Morocco: Techno-cosmopolitanism and Middling Modernism,"*Assemblage* 17 (April 1992). Chapter 4, "Georges Canguilhem: A Vital Rationalist," in *A Vital Rationalist: Georges Canguilhem*, ed. François Delaporte (Zone Books, 1994). Chapter 5, "Artificiality and Enlightenment: From Sociobiology to Biosociality," in *Incorporations*, ed. Jonathan Crary and Sanford Kwinter (Zone Books, 1992). Chapter 6, "Galton's Regret: Of Types and Individuals," in *DNA on Trial: Genetic Identification and Criminal Justice*, ed. Paul Billings (Cold Spring Harbor Press, 1992). Chapter 7, "Fragmentation and Redemption in Late Modernity," in *Knowledge and Society: The Anthropology of Science and Technology*, ed. David Hess and Linda Layne (JAI Press, 1992). Chapter 8, "The Third Culture," *History of the Human Sciences* 7, no. 2 (May 1994).

Essays on the Anthropology of Reason

CHAPTER 1

Science as a Practice:
Ethos, Logos, Pathos

> The moment faith in the God of the ascetic ideal
> is denied, a *new problem arises*: that of the *value*
> of truth . . . the value of truth must for once be
> experimentally *called into question*."
> *(Friedrich Nietzsche, The Genealogy of Morals)*

SITE 1: A SELECT FEW

In the mid-1990s, I attended an international conference on a
cutting-edge topic, assembling leading figures from several disciplines and two continents, held in a basement room at La Villette,
a massive high-modern complex comprising offices, a science museum, and a postmodern park in northeastern Paris. La Villette
was one of the anchors of President Mitterand's project to re-
new eastern Paris, in effect to leave a monumental heritage to his
fourteen-year reign as well as to establish a new axis of specula-
tive development anchored by an opera house at the Bastille,
the biggest library in Europe across the Seine, and La Villette in
the north.[1] Outside lay a rectangular reflecting pond and a giant,
silver-coated globe with interior planetarium. Inside, down an es-
calator, through a library, lay our designated room, well below
ground, shaped as a modified surgical theater, providing an ambi-
ence of artificial light.

We began the conference, starting late, with the usual perfunc-
tory greetings. Each presenter was allotted the standard thirty
minutes; this guideline, it was immediately established, was to be
honored in the breach. One way to pass the time was to ponder
whether successive speakers, as they surpassed their allotted time,
were (a) displaying run-of-the mill arrogance, (b) straightfor-

wardly unprepared and disorganized, or (c) enacting a postmodern performance (it doesn't matter where I start this paper or end it or how long it goes on, I will keep reading until someone stops me, or when I grow weary or simply lose interest). Although the afternoon session began with a reminder that the morning's time schedule had not been respected, the afternoon was much the same. I was told at dinner that the French moderators would never intervene to cut someone off, and that in Italy it was not uncommon for people to mill around and converse among themselves during such events. Finally, one distinguished commentator, who had not attended the first two days of the conference because he had had more pressing business at a government commission and his country house, arrived late, took a seat, and looking harried, began writing out his comments.[2] When the time for his commentary arrived belatedly, he strode to the platform and talked on and on and on—about his own work, not the paper at hand.

The core group at the conference constituted a "network," and in fact networks were one of its main areas of inquiry and discussion. During the breaks a good deal of talk centered around planning the next conference in Berlin. Clearly, the actual event itself was of little or no importance except that it had taken place and could consequently form the basis of a paragraph for a funding proposal submitted to finance the next event. The network had excellent connections to funding commissions, and one could therefore assume that the chances of a positive response were high. The turf was being occupied.

I was irritated and bored. First: bored. In his montage-parody of an autobiography, *Roland Barthes par Roland Barthes*, Roland Barthes includes a photo of himself and three other men sitting at a table each staring off into space while (presumably) another speaks.[3] They are bored. The caption of the photo is "Ennui: La Table Ronde." Boredom, daydreaming, restlessness are common at academic events. Yet the consistent presence of these moods suggests that they are not merely accidental accompaniments to the occasional bad panel, otherwise the speakers would exit in droves and not attend the encore performance of the same script and players (including themselves). As this rarely happens, I take these moods as constitutive elements of such events. They are a significant aspect of what Pierre Bourdieu has named the *habitus* of academic life in the late twentieth century, a tacit but important dimension of that life form's emotional tone, power relations, subjectivations, kinesthetics. As a transdisciplinary form, these occasions might be called the antisymposium, except that such a formulation is too negative; modern forms of power, Michel Foucault taught us, are productive. Modes of interaction, ways of talking, bodily praxis are simultaneously inscribed through institutional custom and enforced through long-term civilizational practices of autopolicing and self-fashioning. To invoke the name of Norbert Elias is to indicate that manners are not marginal to cultural formations. It takes a lot of cultural work to produce a pervasive boredom and inner drift in a filled auditorium of researchers. Even Roland Barthes was disposed to play by the rules.

Then: irritated. The experience at La Villette led me to reflections on some of the constitutive elements of such events, their moods, my reactions. In order to organize these reflections, I use the device of constructing—and thereby contrasting—two "types" (in the Nietzschean-Weberian sense) of science as a practice: (1) the *vigilant virtuoso* (mood = pathos or failed indifference), and (2) the *attentive amateur* (mood = attentiveness or reserved curiosity). These two types are not exhaustive; they do not map the field of contemporary practice. To produce such a map would entail occupying a position I refuse to occupy.

I take the work of Pierre Bourdieu as the most accomplished and successful example of the first type. Bourdieu has carried through not only an organized corpus of monographic investigations, he has achieved a powerful theoretical reflection on his own work. He believes the two to be inextricably bound, a belief that is contestable. I use the conference experience as a takeoff point for these thoughts and not as a metaphor for Bourdieu (although some of his disciples did play a role in the conference). I refract my boredom and irritation into an agonistic relation to Bourdieu's work. My aim is to learn from this exercise, to weigh the effects, the affects, the consequences of such a logically and teleologically consistent attitude. The aim of this engagement is not victory (we are not engaged in sports or war) or revenge (for what?) or refutation (there is much to learn from him, although that is not foregrounded here). Rather, reflecting on my own ethnographic practice, with the help of a set of distinctions developed by Michel Foucault, I assemble the elements of a second and alternate type, one embodying a different practice. My goal is the clarification and cultivation of that practice.

Practice

Although the theme of "practice" has been central to American cultural anthropology for almost a decade now, it is rarely defined with any rigor.[4] Sherry Ortner, in her classic article "Theory in Anthropology Since the Sixties," makes this point: "What is a practice? In principle, the answer to this question is almost unlimited: anything people do. Given the centrality of domination in the model, however, the most significant forms of practice are those with intentional or unintentional political implications. Then again, almost anything people do has such implications. So the study of practice is after all the study of all forms of human action, but from a particular—political—angle."[5] Here I take a different approach, one that is less general and one that takes up practices from a different angle—the ethical rather than the political. How does such a shift reconfigure the practice of knowledge?

Alasdair MacIntyre provides a cogent definition of a practice in his book, *After Virtue*, as "any coherent and complex form of socially established cooperative human activity through which goods internal to that form of activity are realized in the course of trying to achieve those standards of excellence which are appropriate to, and partially definitive of that form of activity, with the result that human powers to achieve excellence, and human conceptions of the ends and goods involved, are systematically extended."[6] The language of the definition is full of terms one rarely, if ever, finds in the social sciences today (form, coherence, excellence, etc.). The reason for this unfamiliarity is that MacIntyre draws these terms from an older vocabulary and tradition,

6

one that exists today as a minor current in moral philosophy, that of the virtues. A virtue, for MacIntyre, is

> an acquired human quality the possession and exercise of which tends to enable us to achieve those goods which are internal to practices and the lack of which effectively presents us from achieving any such goods. The exercise of the virtues is not . . . a means to the end of the good for man. For what constitutes the good for man is a complete human life lived at its best, and the exercise of the virtues is a necessary and central part of such a life, not a mere preparatory exercise to secure such a life. The immediate outcome of the exercise of a virtue is a choice which issues in right action. . . . Virtues are dispositions not only to act in particular ways, but also to feel in particular ways. To act virtuously is not, as Kant was later to think, to act against inclination; it is to act from inclination formed by the cultivation of the virtues. Moral education is an "education sentimentale."[7]

My wager is that returning to this vocabulary will prove to be especially fruitful (to continue the agricultural metaphor) for understanding science as a practice. Although practices and virtues continue to exist, the discourse about them was marginalized by the rise of modern moral philosophy (Kantian, utilitarian, etc.). My advocacy of practice and virtue is an ethnographic and anthropological call to be attentive to existing "minor" practices that escape the dominant discursive trends of theorists of modernity and postmodernity alike.[8] Therefore, somewhat unexpectedly to me at least, it can be taken as yet another critique of modernity. However, my intent is to contribute to what Hans Blumenberg has called "the legitimacy of the modern age," by making some already existing practices and virtues more visible, more available, thereby contributing to their reinvention.

Type I. The Virtuoso of the Rational Will

Pierre Bourdieu chose the following quotation to open his own primer on his own work, *An Invitation to Reflexive Sociology*, tailored to charm and conquer—that is, to civilize—the American social

7

scientific audience/market: "If I had to 'summarize' Wittgenstein, I would say: He made changing the self the prerequisite of all changes."[9] Although it is not evident why Wittgenstein needs to be mentioned at all except as a mark of distinction, the quote draws our attention to the question: What kind of self is it Bourdieu seeks to change? What subject does he want to produce?[10] It also draws our attention to another question: What does he produce?

A. ILLUSIO

Despite the immense complexity and analytic power of Bourdieu's sociological oeuvre, the answer to this question is relatively straightforward. Fundamentally there are only two types of subjects for Bourdieu: those who act in the social world and those who don't. Those who do, do so on condition that fundamentally they are blind to what they are doing, they live in a state of *illusio*, to introduce a fundamental concept in Bourdieu's system. The other possible subject position is the sociologist who studies those who act, those beings who take their lives seriously, those who have "interests." The scientist, through the application of a rigorous method preceded and made possible through the techniques of asceticism applied to the self, frees himself from the embodied practices and organized spaces that produce the *illusio* and sees without illusion what everyone else is doing (they are maximizing their symbolic capital, while mistakenly believing they are leading meaningful lives).[11]

Bourdieu puts it this way: "What I have called *participant objectivation* (and which is not to be mistaken for participant observation) is no doubt the most difficult exercise of all because it requires a break with the deepest and most unconscious adherences and adhesions, those that quite often give the object its very 'interest' for those who study it." Or: "The sociologist unveils the *self-deception* [English in the text], the lies one gives to oneself, collectively kept up and encouraged, which, in every society is at the base of the most sacred values, and for that reason, at the basis of social existence in its entirety."[12] There is one sacrifice required by the sociologist in order to achieve the clarity occasioned by his radical change of consciousness and of ontology: to refuse all social action, all 'interest' in the meaning and/or stakes of social life. Bourdieu, again: "One must in a sense renounce the use of science to intervene in the object which is no doubt at the root of her 'interest' in the object. One must . . . carry out an objectivation which is not merely the partial and reductionist view that one can acquire from within the game, . . . but rather the all-encompassing view that one acquires of a game that can be grasped as such because one has retired from it."[13] For Bourdieu, all social actors are (always) self-interested insofar as they act. However, Bourdieu goes beyond rational actor theory, economism, and sociobiology because he takes great pains to show that self-interest is not a presociological given (he shares the critique of individualism with Louis Dumont and the classic tradition of French sociology); self-interest is defined by the complex structure of overlapping sociological fields to which the actors must be blind in order to act.[14] Bourdieu is absolutely unequivocal that social actors, while acting in terms of their sociologically structured self-interest, can never know what that self-interest is precisely because they must believe in the illusion that they are pursuing something genuinely meaningful in order to act. Only the sociologist is capable of understanding what is really and truly going on; the reason for that success stems from the sacrifice on the altar of truth that the sociologist makes of his own social interests. The sociologist's capacity to perform this miraculous act is based on method, rooted in his claim to be able to occupy a position of exteriority to the social field and the interests at play within it. That miracle is made into a mundane practice through a set of ascetic techniques.

For Bourdieu, this practice of asceticism is shared by all scientists. He says: "Indeed, I hold that, all the scholastic discussions about the distinctiveness of the human sciences not withstanding, the human sciences are subject to the same rules that apply to all sciences. . . . I am struck, when I speak with my friends who are chemists, physicians, or neurobiologists, by the similarities between their practice and that of a sociologist. The typical day of a sociologist, with its experimental groping, statistical analysis, reading of scholarly papers, and discussion with colleagues, looks very much like that of an ordinary scientist to me."[15] Although

9

there are a number of debatable points made in the quotation (are the experimental gropings really the same in sociology and biochemistry? Is all science holistic? Why hasn't Bourdieu's science become paradigmatic? etc.), none is more so than Bourdieu's central point that the sciences are unified. Or more accurately, ultimately there are no sciences in the plural, there is only science—in the singular. If there is only one true scientific practice, then it follows that there is only one scientific vocation and one scientific ethos.

B. INDIFFERENCE

Where does this manly bracketing of social life, this methodically relentless self-purifying, this self-imposed obsessive tracking down of any and all residual *illusio*, leave Bourdieu? He is, as always, unflinching in drawing conclusions: it leads him into a state of utter indifference. "To understand the notion of interest, it is necessary to see that it is opposed not only to that of disinterestedness or gratuitousness but also to that of *indifference*. To be indifferent is to be unmoved by the game: like Buridan's donkey, this game makes no difference to me. Indifference is an axiological state, an ethical state of non-preference as well as a state of knowledge in which I am not capable of differentiating the stakes proposed."[16] Bourdieu invokes the Stoic goal of ataraxy (*ataraxia*, not being troubled). *Illusio* is the very opposite of ataraxy: it is to be invested, taken in and by the game. To be interested is to accord a given social game that that which happens in it matters, that its stakes are important (another word with the same root as interest) and worth pursuing. One can and should—qua social scientist— achieve *ataraxia*, indifference, about anything and everything. Not to be taken in, not to care, these are the necessary conditions for scientific practice.

What are the consequences, the rewards, the meaning—the value—of Bourdieu's hard-won indifference? He closes his inaugural speech at the Collège de France, "Leçon sur la leçon" with a peroration that brings his distinctive style to its apogee. He says:

> The paradoxical enterprise which consists in using a position of authority in order to say with authority what it means to speak with au-

thority, so as to give a lesson, but a lesson in liberty with respect to all other lessons, would be simply inconsequential, almost self-destructive, if the very ambition to construct a science of belief didn't presuppose a belief in science. Nothing is less cynical, less machiavellian, than those paradoxical proclamations who announce or denounce the principle of power which they exercise. There is no sociologist who would take the risk of destroying the thin veil of faith or of bad faith which makes the charm of all institutional pieties, if he didn't have the faith in the possibility and the necessity of universalizing the freedom in regard to institutions which sociology has procured for itself; if he did not believe in the liberating virtues of that which is the least illegitimate of symbolic powers, that of science, especially when that science takes the form of a science of symbolic powers capable of restoring to social subjects the mastery of false transcendentals which *la méconnaissance* never stops creating and recreating."[17]

Bourdieu professes his belief in science; he defends that belief by arguing for its potential universality. Sociology triumphant will restore a "mastery of false transcendentals" which society constantly re-instates, as it is its function to do. Were sociology ever to triumph, were we ever all to become sociologists—at that moment, what would happen to society?

For Bourdieu, *illusio* and faith are the preconditions of society. Society could not exist without an ontologically rooted *epistemological* blindness. Given his premises, he is thoroughly consistent in arriving at an understanding in which humans are universally blind to the deep meaning of their own acts, a stance Alan Pred calls "epistemologically rooted ontological blindness."[18] From his position of achieved indifference, Bourdieu does not despise them, but expresses instead a kind of—unmotivated—solidarity with their human plight. His position is unmotivated in the sense that there is no scientific reason to sympathize—one could just as consistently adopt any one of a series of attitudes, for example Claude Lévi-Strauss's "view from afar" that expresses a kind of resigned contempt, a slightly tempered retake of the utter scorn that he had asserted forty years earlier for anyone who would be interested in a "shop-girl's web of subjectivity." We see this ethical, emotional and eventual political impasse, perhaps a sign of a

11

surviving shred of Bourdieu's own *illusio*, in a short, two-page caution "to the reader" with which Bourdieu opens a collective work
entitled *La Misère du monde*. The first-person accounts of suffering,
hurt, and degradations of ordinary life in France contained in the
volume, Bourdieu instructs the reader, have "been organized in
order to obtain from the reader his accord to give them a gaze
(*regard*) as *comprehensive* as that which the exigencies of the scientific method impose on them." It is not sufficient, the reader is
reminded, to quote Spinoza's precept, "Don't deplore, don't
laugh, don't detest, but understand," if one does not insure the
means to respect it. A rigorous sociological science provides those
means. Nonetheless, how could one not feel, after all, Bourdieu
observes, a certain "uneasiness" having published these private
observations (*propos*) which had been given in confidence, even
though the purpose of collecting them was never hidden from
those that gave them. Not surprisingly, this uneasiness can only be
addressed, if not entirely quelled, through taking every precau-
tion that they not be misunderstood, that there be no *détourne-
ments de sens*. Surprisingly, Bourdieu apologizes for the possibility
that he risks sounding clinical though he never explains precisely
what is wrong with sounding clinical, since "whether one likes it or
not," these people are, and can only be, "objects" for the sociologist.[19] He is, in point of fact, being perfectly clinical, and given
his diagnosis, appropriately so.

Bourdieu's pages *are* unquestionably tinged with sympathy and
solidarity for the people he analyzes. Bourdieu's personal sentiments, sincere and noble though they may be, however, have no
scientific role to play in his system. They remain private, personal,
accidental—ultimately unreflective and unreflected. His sentimental education has been to deny the legitimacy of all sentiments; rather, he has learned the lesson of *illusio* and indifference, of a certain ascetic scientific practice, one he teaches and
practices brilliantly.[20] But the brilliance of his analysis illuminates
his own practice (as well as those of the social actors he sees as
shrouded in *illusio*). It is for that reason they are also informed by
the (self-imposed ascetic) distance of what Hans Blumenberg has
called the "missionary and didactic pathos," characteristic of a cer-

tain tradition of French thought. Against the grain of his own system, Bourdieu does sympathize, does find the pervasive reproduction of social inequalities, which he documents so scrupulously, both fascinating and intolerable, he *does* respect his subjects—that is clearly why he focuses book after book on these themes. However, he "knows" better and therefore must engage in the constant battle to overcome these sentiments, so as to become, like Buridan's ass, indifferent. Hence, his (unrecognized) pathos. An ethos of logos without (an accounted for) pathos yields virtuosity, not virtue.

Site II. Philia or Friendship

I had been bored and irritated at La Villette. Why? The causes are multiple: partially poor socialization (I don't go to enough of these events), partially temperament (restless and exigent). Partially because I knew that there were other ways of doing things. Commenting on a draft of this paper, a friend pointed out to me that in the same passage that I quoted earlier, Barthes also says that the boredom that used to dominate his existence had gradually decreased, thanks "to work and to friends."[21]

I propose that a primary site of thinking is friendship (*philia*). Such a formulation sounds strange, as friendship is a relationship and not a physical place. Today, we have lecture rooms and conference rooms and meeting rooms and classrooms and offices and studies; the Romans had rooms for friends. In the ancient world, friendship figured in different ways as an essential component of the good life (*eudaimonia*), a prime site of human flourishing. Conceptions and practices of philia took many different forms, from the honor-based culture described in the *Iliad*, through the classic Greek tragedies and philosophy. The *locus classicus* of this tradition is Aristotle's *Nicomachean Ethics*. In Book 8, Aristotle writes: "Friendship is a virtue . . . most necessary with a view to living. For without friends no one would choose to live, though he had all other goods; even rich men and those in possession of office and of dominating power are thought to need friends most of all. . . . For with friends men are most able both to think and to act." Aristotle distinguished among three kinds of friends: friendships based on utility, those based on pleasure, and finally "the good." The first has no doubt always been the most common. Utility/philia relationships are ones in which self-advantage figures prominently for both parties. Consequently, Aristotle observed, when the motives or occasions of mutual profit are loosened, such temporary friendships are readily dissolved. For Aristotle, there were a great number of different types of these utilitarian relationships, and, good observer that he was, he detailed them at length.

Today, the daily life of the sciences is saturated with personal ties which serve diverse functions. It is sometimes forgotten that mutual advantage needs to be identified and negotiated as much as anything else. Hence, professional self-interest, the accumulation of symbolic capital and the like, is more than a question of predefined roles or "objective interests" or even dispositions, although those dimensions constitute the preconditions for utility/philia. The utility/philia dimension remains largely unexplored. Observation suggests it is a contemporary site of ethical reflection where goods are balanced. It is thematized more in soap operas and talk shows than in scholarly books.

Friendships based on pleasure (of commensality or bodily acts, from erotic to athletic) are probably less cultivated, although certain pleasures are included in professional circles. Conventions are among the biggest sectors of the American economy. The face-to-face encounters, repeated with some regularity over time, while hard to justify in quantifiable economic terms, clearly continue to be valued, probably for reasons that could not be explicitly defended by corporations and universities, but which do, indeed, have some value in the terms we have been using.

For Aristotle, the highest form of friendship is the philosopher's philia. "Perfect friendship is the friendship of men who are good and alike in virtue; for those wish well alike to each other qua good, and they are good in themselves." The best friendships require time and a long familiarity to develop and solidify. "A wish for friendship," Aristotle writes, "may arise quickly, but friendship does not."[22] Friendship is mutual, social, and quasi-public. It is ecstatic in that its practice draws one out and toward a friend.

14

Philia primes the bond, the among and the between. Marilyn Strathern has shown how rare it is in modern Western societies to conceive of anything other than individuals and contractual relationships.[23]

How to situate the philia-site? "Imagine for a moment a marginalized intellectual, who has been engaged in philosophy and the intellectual life since his teens, and is almost entirely lacking in political power or influence, sitting down to determine what the best kind of life and the best kind of polis are. Imagine that and you have to a large degree imagined Aristotle in his ethics and politics class in the Lyceum. For Aristotle entered Plato's Academy at the age of 17, staying there for twenty years. . . . Moreover, he was a metic—a resident alien—in Athens and was barred from playing an active role in Athenian political life."[24] He did, however, find the space to do a good deal of participant observation before leaving Athens rather urgently, in order, or so the legend goes, to aid the Athenians from committing a second crime against philosophy.

First the Stoics, and then the Christians displaced friendship from the center of the good life. For the Stoics, friendship was one of the local and contingent relationships from whose ties they sought to be released in order to establish a connection to the cosmos, the universal. Although the place of friendship in Christianity is a complex one, while remaining a minor good it was theorized as a danger to the faithful's (often a monk's) primary attachment to God. Friendships became inherently triangular. Though there are occasional references to friendship in the philosophic tradition (e.g., Montaigne), friendship basically became a "marginal practice" in the sense of losing its philosophic centrality.[25] Today, it is largely seen as therapeutic. Against that trend, I view philia as an ethical and epistemological *practice*.

Type II. The Attentive Amateur: Cosmopolitan Curiosity

In his last works, Michel Foucault produced a provocative framework for analyzing ethics. Ethics, for Foucault, is "the kind of relationship you ought to have with yourself, *rapport à soi,* . . . which

15

determines how the individual is supposed to constitute himself as a moral subject of his own actions."[26] Foucault identifies four distinct aspects in ethical self-constitution: ethical substance, modes of subjectivation, ethical work (askesis in the sense of training or exercise), or telos. This scheme was developed by Foucault to further refine his interest in sexuality in relation to the "care of the self," how the subject ordered his sexuality in a general economy of the philosophic life. My interest here is scientific practice and the care of the self, the elements at play in the ethical elaboration of science as a vocation. I use Foucault's distinctions, with this major reorientation of content, as an experimental means to explore what is in play and what is at stake.

1. Ethical Substance. "What is the aspect of myself or my behavior which is concerned with moral conduct."[27]

For Bourdieu, the ethical substance is the will. The will is that aspect that must be mastered for science to be possible and it is only through science that such mastery is possible.[28]

In contrast, I take the *ethical substance*, the prime material of moral conduct, to be reflective curiosity. Here I follow a long tradition stemming from Aristotle—whose *Metaphysics* opens with the famous proposition, "All men by nature desire to know"—on through Hans Blumenberg, who provides, in his *The Legitimacy of the Modern Age*, the fullest description of what he calls "the trial of theoretical curiosity," in Western philosophy (including an erudite commentary on the history of interpretations and criticisms of Aristotle's opening line).[29] Blumenberg, like Aristotle, sees curiosity as a natural disposition (shared with animals), but one which takes a distinctive reflective or mediated form in humans. This historically shaped form is the ethical substance.

It is precisely its open-endedness that makes reflected curiosity an ethical substance. As Aristotle argued in Book 2 of *The Nicomachean Ethics*, virtues (and the dispositions that make them possible) are neither passions nor faculties: "For we are neither called good nor bad, nor praised nor blamed, for the simple capacity of feeling the passions; again we have the faculties by nature, but we are not made good or bad by nature." Virtues then are a state of character which "makes a man good and which makes him do his own work well."[30] Ethical substance, understood in this way, is not a potential which could be actualized, as that would be too naturalistic, but rather a disposition to be shaped.[31] This intellectual disposition, if formed by the right practices and cultivated in the right institutions, can become a virtue or, equally, given other contexts and other dispositions, it has the possibility to take a degraded form—either a deficient state in which it withers away or in an excessive manner in which it seeks complete autonomy. It is precisely that malleability which makes the dispositions the material of intellectual and ethical virtues. Seen in this light, it is possible to imagine a history of science and philosophy as a long series of experiments in determining the extent of the dispositions' malleability, their elaboration and their enduring possibility of corruption.[32]

One advantage of choosing reflected curiosity as the ethical substance is that it is at least partially shared by both the person studying science and the scientists themselves. Hence, the inquiry begins on the basis of a shared disposition. This commonality does not mean that what molecular biologists and anthropologists, for example, do with this disposition (the kind of work they perform on it, the forms they give it, the norms and institutions within which they practice) is identical—clearly they aren't. Nonetheless, a tacit sharing of curiosity makes possible, even encourages, an exchange, a situation that encourages a mutual reflection on each other's practices. It follows that the choice of reflective curiosity as the ethical substance is itself an ethical one.[33]

2. Mode of Subjectivation. "The way in which the individual establishes his relation to the rule and acknowledges oneself to be a member of the group that accepts it, declares adherence to it out loud, and silently preserves it as a custom. But one can practice it too as an heir to a spiritual tradition that one has the responsibility of maintaining or reviving."[34]

Bourdieu's scientist freely takes up a kind of "this-wordly *mysticism*," in Max Weber's phrase. The "inner worldly mystic," Weber writes, "is in the world and accommodates to its orders, but only to gain a certainty of grace in opposition to the world by resisting the temptation to take the ways of the world seriously."[35] The social-scientific "this-worldly mystic" is a man of abiding conviction. He believes society has *a* meaning; to seize it, he has to stay close to human actors, as the habitus is always specific, yet he has to be released from society's hold through scientific askesis in order to seize that meaning.

One could link experience and experiment, ethics and epistemology, in a more exploratory manner. In 1916, John Dewey provided an excellent characterization of such a stance: "An intellectual integrity, an impartiality and detachment, which is maintained only in seclusion is unpleasantly reminiscent of other identifications of virtue with the innocence of ignorance. To place knowledge where it arises and operates in experience is to know that, as it arose because of the troubles of man, it is confirmed in reconstructing the conditions which occasioned those troubles. Genuine intellectual integrity is found in experimental knowing. Until this lesson is fully learned, it is not safe to dissociate knowledge from experiment nor experiment from experience."[36] And of course this lesson has not been learned.

In my recent ethnographic work in France and in the United States with molecular biologists, I explicitly addressed the question of who I was, what my affiliations were, and what commitments I had with the scientists I was engaging. During my ethnographic work at Roche Molecular Systems I explained that as a citizen I was concerned and interested in ethical and political implications of the Human Genome Initiative; as an anthropologist I was attempting to evaluate claims coming from genetically oriented physical anthropologists about human behavior; as a professor I thought I ought to know more about how the lines between the academy and industry had changed the practice of science. Although presenting myself as an ethnographer, I never pretended to be entirely an observer; consequently I constantly engaged these scientists in discussions and debates, which they welcomed and from which I learned what to ask. In France, during my work at the CEPH, I was invited in by Daniel Cohen, the institution's driving force, as a "philosophic observer." Cohen wanted to experiment with ways to introduce a "social" interlocutor into his lab without introducing ethics committees, which he saw as too pre-emptive. This slot of floating inquirer—watching and commenting on an institution very much engaged in thinking through and acting on such issues as the place of national science within a new international arena, which paradigms to pursue for multifactorial genetic diseases, and the ethical and strategic role of patenting, all unresolved but pressing issues—suited me. The extraordinary outpouring of views, reflections, demonstrations, and debates to which I became privy arose to a large extent because I explicitly presented myself in a tradition based on both philosophic questioning and empirical inquiry. The "social field" of the scientists in both instances was in a state of change, as was my own. Making that state of uncertainty and flux explicit acknowledged and encouraged reflection on the different practices we were both engaged in.

My "mode of subjectivation" aligned me with those who start with the "native's point of view." It separated me from that tradition, however, insofar as the natives did not have a stable point of view but were themselves engaged in questioning their allegiances, their dispositions. Their culture was in the making. Further, it was partially my culture. Their self-questioning over how to shape their scientific practice, the limits of their ability to do so, partially overlapped with my own scientific practice. I attempted to foreground both the overlap and the difference—and, over time, to make this emerging situation both a topic of curiosity and a mode of inquiry.

3. Ethical work. "The work that one performs on oneself, not only in order to bring one's conduct into compliance with a given rule, but to attempt to transform oneself into the ethical subject of one's behavior."

For Bourdieu, in order "to become the ethical subject of one's behavior" one must overcome *illusio*. The work that one must perform to achieve this overcoming is participant objectivation. The participation is at the level of the self, a constant self-*vigilance*, a

19

methodical, relentless hunting down of (social) life-enabling mystifications. The constant danger is to be naive, to be taken in. The self achieves its ethical status through two steps: the objectivation of society as a totality and the cognitive relationship it affects to that (constructed) objectivation. By so doing, one "brings one's conduct into compliance with a given rule" and "transforms oneself into the ethical subject of one's behavior."

The contrastive challenge is to overcome *ressentiment*. The work that one performs is participant observation. But not all participant observation will do. First, the participation is at the level of a relationship between subjects. These subjects are not identical but they are not radically different either. Second, the observation, at least in part, takes as its object the process of construction of that intersubjective relationship. At no point, therefore, is the curious participant-observer either totally external to or totally identified with the field of study. *Ressentiment* requires, demands, fabricates, and defends clearly drawn boundaries between subjects and objects in order to operate. Hence a liminal placement provides a preliminary defense. The danger is losing the balance, tipping too far toward the subjective side or the objective side. The ethical task is finding the mean. As Aristotle argued, there are no rules for achieving this mean; it is a question of experience and practical activity, the work of keeping track of the just proportion of things.

Today, the critique of *ressentiment* is conspicuously present in some branches of feminism. Some feminist philosophers identify two dangers they find prevalent (often most acutely among other feminists). First, adopting a politics of ressentiment fixes subject positions and boundaries between subjects. Wendy Brown, in her book *States of Injury*, writes that "ressentiment fixes the identities of the injured and the injuring as social positions and codifies as well the meanings of their actions against all possibilities of indeterminacy, ambiguity, and struggle for resignification or repositioning."[37] This fixing is detrimental to forming alliances and impoverishes the political imagination, blocking others' modes of subjectivation. Second, rigid boundary maintenance, and the cursed couple of demonization/cupidization, leads to the inability to affirm. Marion Tapper, in an essay, "Ressentiment and

Power: Some Reflections on Feminist Practices," develops this line of argument, showing how a politics of victimage yields a politics of moral superiority.[38] This politics produces, among other things, an inability to admire and respect, to the extent it is their due, those one is seeking to understand or to change. Following Nietzsche, she argues that this demonization and its intimately associated contempt apply—reflexively and doggedly—to the knower as well as the known.

Although the identification of these critical points of ressentiment's entry into politics is pertinent, they require a twist to fit the ethical-epistemological practice. It is in the carefully chosen fieldwork site that one acquires and tests a sense of the ethical and intellectual limits of what is actual and what is possible, of virtue and corruption, of domination and growth of capacities. Every situation is historically and culturally overdetermined. Part of the work of fieldwork is to identify the particularities and generalities of the situation, of the contingent and less contingent—and to be concerned with both sides of these pairs. The ethical work is concerned less with being vigilant and more with an attentiveness, a reserved and reflected curiosity about what form of life is being made. It is through fieldwork, through experiential experimentation, that one establishes "partial connections," reflects on them, gives them an appropriate form.

Such "normatively oriented" fieldwork discovered arenas in which the scientists themselves expressed irritation and frustration about aspects of scientific work they considered violations of their practice; some instances embodied tensions, others corruptions, others betrayals. The scientists certainly assumed they were engaged in "normed" activity and were quite appreciative of being systematically questioned about it. In some instances, they lacked a vocabulary to identify what "troubled" them, in others they were quite eloquent. In both the United States and France, it became clear to me that I was not expected to play an expert role of analyzing them sociologically, nor a therapeutic role of helping them "work through" problems, nor a denunciatory role of identifying malevolent forces and actors, but a problematizing role, one in which having an observer status allowed a certain overview of the

21

situation, including its fluidity. Such a mode of subjectivation requires the ethical work of being attentive to one's own ressentiments, of claiming neither mastery nor ignorance, of publicly balancing identification and distance.

4. Telos. "That activity in which one finds the self. An action is not only moral in itself, in its singularity; it is also moral in its circumstantial integration and by virtue of the place it occupies in a pattern of conduct."

Bourdieu's sociological subject attains the universal by achieving separation from all particularity and action, a self freed from *illusio.* The aim is *mastery.* The goal of the "dominated members of the dominated class" (Bourdieu's term for intellectuals) is discursive mastery. The failed form of discursive mastery is, as Nietzsche saw, "spiritual revenge." The successful form is the state of higher indifference toward the world, the overcoming of suffering understood as passion, as a way of life.

As long as one accepts the equation of human science with natural science—as Bourdieu does—then the search for technical mastery of society and self appears plausible. It appears plausible, and not in need of a defense, as long as one ignores the work of the social studies of science and technology and feminism in the last two decades on the status of "nature," "society," and "self." Even then, those who accept the equation must confront the Weberian line of argument most recently put forward by the philosopher Gyorgy Markus. In an incisive article entitled "Why Is There No Hermeneutics of the Natural Sciences?" Markus concludes that there is no such practice because there is no need for one. The natural sciences have succeeded in evacuating meaning from their productions. Markus's conclusion is directly in line with Weber's claim that the logic of rationalization had in principle disenchanted the world, but provided no answers to questions of general cultural significance. Growing technical mastery and specialization in the natural sciences has yielded both control and a progressive narrowing of meaning.[39] In a strict sense, there is no *self*-questioning *within* molecular biology. From time to time, there are debates about the ends to which results could be put, political projects that might be dangerous or beneficial; there are occasional discussions about the composition (gender, race, class) of the social body of scientists, but the normative parameters of the textual and nondiscursive practices of sciences like molecular biology are not in question, however fluid they may be in daily life. The relation of molecular biologists toward their objects of study may well be open to criticism, but not on the grounds that they are characterized by *ressentiment*. Most, perhaps all, of the practicing molecular biologists I have worked with accepted these limitations, some quite consciously—that was one of the reasons they were curious about my work. When natural scientists stop doing science and start producing "worldviews," *ressentiment* and *illusio* run rampant.

As historians such as Steve Shapin have shown, there is a history of the creation, stabilization, and maintenance of the figure of the natural scientist, but that history shows a socially successful displacement of self-examination into "experiments" and "nature." Many dream of replicating this historical feat in the human sciences, but they have never been successful in achieving and stabilizing the institutional and cultural conditions required to authorize and enforce such a consensus. It appears to be the case that it would only be through political means that such a consolidation could take place. Then mastery would be complete.

In my formulation, the telos of a reflectively curious practice of human science is a form of *bildung*, a kind of individual and collective self-formation or *lebensführung* (life-regulation), a type of care and cultivation. Such a *bildung* turns on being attentive to the plurality and dignity of beings (humans and others) as well as the limits of that pluralism and dignity. It is not a classical *bildung*, insofar as that tradition took the textual and cultural canon to be already fully identified and the arts of interpretation already codified or sought that stability as an end. It is worth noting that how stable or hegemonic the identification and codification of the canon is—or was—is an open question, a topic of debate, a site of interpretation or struggle. The proposed *bildung* does not take the form of a high revolutionary modernism; it rejects the practice that proceeds as if it were either possible or desirable to start *de novo* as well as the one that seeks to totally remake the self and/or society.

The contrastive type might be called a "cosmopolitan amateur." Although "amateur" is a somewhat clumsy term, it points to a practice that does not take mastery as its goal. The amateur stands back from the virtuosity of the expert. Once again, its excellence lies in the mean. Finally, the telos of the second type is not only amateur but cosmopolitan. A cosmopolitan ethos entails a perspective on knowledge, ethics, and politics that is simultaneously local and global, native and foreign. At one level, this claim is quite commonsensical and follows directly from the voluminous literature on globalization (market, media, bureaucracy, arms trade, development, etc.). However, the "state of the world" can always be taken up, problematized in diverse ways.

Molecular biology, for example, has taken up the current conjuncture through an increased use of electronic means of communication, of data storage, of internationally coordinated projects like the human (and other organisms) genome mapping projects. The circulation and coordination of knowledge has never been more rapid or more international. Articulating and sustaining these goals is extremely expensive. Heads of major laboratories may well spend the majority of their time raising money, making contacts and forging alliances. The appearance in the last two decades of "start-up" biotechnology companies funded by venture capital and stock offerings, first in the United States and increasingly in Asia, India, and Europe, has reshaped both the financing of research and (probably) its directions. Capital is international. While the principle of the international status of science has been in place for a long time, the form that it is taking in the biomedical sciences today is quite distinct. What kind of scientific life is it that is constantly traveling, constantly negotiating over resources, constantly engaged in competitive claims of priority, competing in multiple arenas? Is this the end of an era of a scientific type? Or is it an acceleration, a hypermodernity, pushing the type to its limits, opening new possibilities of beneficial and appropriate control of things?

The questions one might well pose to the molecular biologist today have a refracted resonance for those of us involved in a different practice. Will it be possible to cultivate yet more complicated participation in larger and more elaborate projects, enabling the development of capacities we barely knew about previously, while minimizing our imprecations with new systems of domination? Are we thrusting toward some threshold of scale where hybrid networks of things and people, micro- and macro-knowledges and powers, makes the very idea of practice archaic? Although I doubt the answer is "yes" to the last question, the only way to find out is to experiment by putting the "circumstantial integration" of our current practices into new "patterns of conduct." The challenge is to find the means.

NOTES

1. Anthony Vidler, *The Architectural Uncanny: Essays in the Modern Unhomely* (Cambridge, Mass.: MIT Press, 1992).

2. This person was not Pierre Bourdieu, as a number of readers have assumed.

3. Roland Barthes, *Roland Barthes par Roland Barthes* (Paris: Editions du Seuil, 1975), p. 28.

4. Many thanks for friendly help from Joao Biehl and James Faubion. As well from John Zu, Nadine Tonio, Mike Panisitti, Natasha Schull, Andrew Lakoff, Adriyana Petryna, and Rebecca Lomov. Teaching, when one has such students, is a pleasure, a utility, a good, and a privilege. Hubert Dreyfus, Robert Bellah, and Roger Friedland provided helpful commentary as well.

5. Sherry B. Ortner, "Theory in Anthropology since the Sixties," *Comparative Studies in Society and History* 26, no. 1 (1984): 149.

6. Alasdair MacIntyre, *After Virtue* (South Bend, Ind.: University of Notre Dame Press, 1981), p. 175. My thinking on practices has been shaped by many conversations with James Faubion. See his "Introduction" to *Rethinking the Subject* (Boulder, Colo.: Westview Press, 1994).

7. MacIntyre, *After Virtue*, pp. 178, 140.

8. Hubert Dreyfus and I used the term "marginal practices" in *Michel Foucault: Beyond Structuralism and Hermeneutics* (Chicago: University of Chicago Press, 1982).

9. In Pierre Bourdieu and Loic Wacquant, *An Introduction to Reflexive Sociology* (Chicago: University of Chicago Press, 1992), p. 61.

10. Joao Biehl here as elsewhere indicates to me the psychoanalytic resonances of the passages and interpretations given. For example, the discussion of "ego-ideal and ideal ego," in Jacques Lacan, *The Seminar, Book I* (New York: Norton, 1991; orig. 1975), pp. 129–42.

11. On this point, see H. Dreyfus and P. Rabinow, "Is a Science of Meaningful Action Possible?" in Craig Calhoun, ed., *Bourdieu: Critical Perspectives* (Chicago: University of Chicago Press, 1993). A parallel (and thoroughly elaborated) overall line of argument about Bourdieu's work is made by Luc Boltanski, a former Bourdieu student, in *De la justification: Les economies de la grandeur* (Paris: Editions Gallimard, 1991).

12. Pierre Bourdieu, *Leçon sur la leçon* (Paris: Les Editions de Minuit, 1982), p. 33. (My translation.)

13. Bourdieu and Wacquant, *Introduction*, pp. 253, 259.

14. Louis Dumont, *Essays on Individualism: Modern Ideology in Anthropological Perspective* (Chicago: University of Chicago Press, 1986; orig. 1983).

15. Bourdieu and Wacquant, *Introduction*, p. 185.

16. Ibid., pp. 115–17.

17. Bourdieu, *Leçon sur la leçon*, p. 56.

18. Alan Pred, personal communication.

19. Pierre Bourdieu, *La Misère du monde* (Paris: Editions du Seuil, 1993), p. 8.

20. The historical grounding of this pathos is captured by Jurgen Habermas: "The empirical-analytic sciences develop their theories in a self-understanding that automatically generates continuity with the beginnings of philosophical thought. For both are committed to a theoretical attitude that frees those who take it from dogmatic association with the natural interests of life and their irritating influences; and both share the cosmological intention of describing the universe theoretically in its law-like order, just as it is. . . . The sciences borrow two elements from the philosophic heritage: the methodological meaning of the theoretical attitude and the basic ontological assumption of a structure of the world independent of the knower. . . . On the other hand, however, they have abandoned the connection theoria and cosmos. . . . What was once supposed to comprise the practical efficacy of theory has now fallen prey to methodological prohibitions. The conception of theory as a process of cultivation of the person has become apocryphal. Today it appears to us that the mimetic conformity of the soul to the proportions of the universe, which seemed accessible to contemplation, had taken only theoretical knowledge into the service of the internalization of norms and thus estranged it from its legitimate task." See *Knowledge and Human Interests* (Boston: Beacon Press, 1971; orig. 1968), pp. 303–4.

21. Thanks to Joao Biehl for returning from Brazil.

22. Aristotle, *Ethics*, Book 10. See Rabinow, *Reflections on Fieldwork in Morocco* (Berkeley: University of California Press, 1977), for one use of these ideas.

23. Marilyn Strathern, *After Nature: English Kinship in the Late Twentieth Century* (Cambridge U.K.: Cambridge University Press, 1992).

24. C.D.E. Reeve, *Practices of Reason: Aristotle's Nicomachean Ethics* (Oxford: Clarendon Press, 1992), p. 195.

25. On marginality, see Dreyfus and Rabinow, *Michel Foucault: Beyond Structuralism and Hermeneutics*, pp. 262–63. Joao Biehl points to the omission of the Judaic tradition.

26. Michel Foucault, "On the Genealogy of Ethics," in ibid., p. 238.

27. This and the following definitions are from ibid.

28. Many thanks to Mike Panisitti and Rebecca Lemov on this point. Scientists who study things don't have objects defined by *illusio*. Do networks have *illusio* ?

29. Hans Blumenberg, *Legitimacy*, For the thirteenth century nominalists, "The first sentence of Aristotle's *Metaphysics* could have been modified so as to say that man has to strive for knowledge, not indeed by nature, but as the being who is exposed to this uncertain world, whose ground plan is hidden from him" (p. 347).

30. Aristotle, *The Nicomachean Ethics*, Bk. 2, in Richard McKeon, ed., *Introduction to Aristotle* (New York: Random House, n.d.), pp. 339–41.

31. On the distinction of potentiality and disposition, see L. A. Kosman, "Being Properly Affected: Virtues and Feelings in Aristotle's Ethics," in Amelie Rorty, ed., *Essays on Aristotle's Ethics* (Berkeley: University of California Press, 1980), p. 111.

32. The relation of the generality of the virtues and the particular ways in which they are given specific forms is treated at length in Martha Nussbaum, "Non-Relative Values: An Aristotelian View," in M. Nussbaum and Amartya Sen, eds., *The Quality of Life* (Oxford: Clarendon Paperbacks, 1993). On the malleability and its limits, see Michel Foucault, "What Is Enlightenment?" in Paul Rabinow, ed., *The Foucault Reader* (New York: Pantheon Books, 1984).

33. Both Gary Downey and I adopt something like this starting point in our work with scientists.

34. Michel Foucault, *The Uses of Pleasure: The History of Sexuality*, vol. 2 (New York: Pantheon Books), p. 28.

35. Max Weber, "Religious Rejections of the World," in H. H. Gerth and C. Wright Mills, *From Max Weber* (New York: Oxford University Press, 1946), p. 326.

36. John Dewey, "Introduction," in *Essays in Experimental Logic* (New York: Dover Books, 1953; orig. 1916), pp. 73–74.

37. Wendy Brown, *States of Injury, Power and Freedom in Late Modernity* (Princeton, N.J.: Princeton University Press, 1995), p. 27.

38. Marion Tapper, "Ressentiment and Power: Some Reflections on Feminist Practice," in Paul Patton, ed., *Nietzsche, Feminism and Political Theory* (London and New York: Routledge, 1993).

39. Gyorgy Markus, "Why Is There No Hermeneutics of the Natural Sciences? Some Preliminary Theses," *Science in Context* 1 (1987): 29.

CHAPTER 2

Representations Are Social Facts: Modernity and Post-Modernity in Anthropology

BEYOND EPISTEMOLOGY

In his influential book *Philosophy and the Mirror of Nature*, Richard Rorty argues that epistemology as the study of mental representations arose in a particular historical epoch, the seventeenth century, developed in a specific society, that of Europe; and eventually triumphed in philosophy by being closely linked to the professional claims of one group, nineteenth-century German professors of philosophy.[1] For Rorty, this turn was not a fortuitous one: "The desire for a theory of knowledge is a desire for constraints— a desire to find 'foundations' to which one might cling, frameworks beyond which one must not stray, objects which impose themselves, representations which cannot be gainsaid" (315). Radicalizing Thomas Kuhn, Rorty portrays our obsession with epistemology as an accidental, but eventually sterile, turning in Western culture.

Pragmatic and American, Rorty's book has a moral: modern professional philosophy represents the "triumph of the quest for certainty over the quest for reason" (61). The chief culprit in this melodrama is Western philosophy's concern with epistemology, the equation of knowledge with internal representations and the correct evaluation of those representations. Philosophers, Rorty argues, have crowned their discipline the queen of the sciences. This coronation rests on their claim to be the specialists on universal problems and their ability to provide us with a sure foundation for all knowledge. Philosophy's realm is the mind; its privileged insights establish its claim to be the discipline that judges all other disciplines. This conception of philosophy is, however, a recent historical development. For the Greeks there was no sharp division between external reality and internal representations. Unlike Aristotle, Descartes' conception of knowing rests on having correct representations in an internal space—the mind. "The novelty," Rorty says, "was the notion of a single inner space in which bodily and perceptual sensations (confused ideas of sense and imagination in Descartes' phrase), mathematical truths, moral rules, the idea of God, moods of depression, and the rest of what we now call 'mental' were objects of quasi-observation" (50). Although not all of these elements were new ones, Descartes successfully combined them into a new problematic, setting aside Aristotle's concept of reason as a grasp of universals: beginning in the seventeenth century, knowledge became internal, representational, and judgmental. Modern philosophy was born when a knowing subject endowed with consciousness and its representational contents became the central problem for thought, the paradigm of all knowing.

The modern notion of epistemology, then, turns on the clarification and judgment of the subject's representations: "To know is to represent accurately what is outside the mind; so to understand the possibility and nature of knowledge is to understand the way in which the mind is able to construct such representations. Philosophy's eternal concern is to be a general theory of representations, a theory which will divide culture up into areas which represent reality well, those which represent it less well, and those which do not represent it at all (despite their pretense of doing so)" (3). The knowledge arrived through the examination of representations about "reality" and "the knowing subject" would be universal.

It was only at the end of the Enlightenment that the fully elaborated conception of philosophy as the judge of all possible knowledge appeared and was canonized in the work of Immanuel Kant. Rorty argues, "The eventual demarcation of philosophy from science was made possible by the notion that philosophy's core was a 'theory of knowledge,' a theory distinct from the sciences because it was their foundation" (132). Kant established as a priori the Cartesian claim that we have certainty only about ideas: "by taking everything we say to be about something we have constituted, [Kant] made it possible for epistemology to be thought of as a foundational science. . . . He thus enabled philosophy professors to see themselves as presiding over a tribunal of pure reason, able to determine whether other disciplines were staying within the legal limits set by the 'structure' of their subject matters" (139).

As a discipline whose proper activity is grounding claims to knowledge, philosophy was developed by nineteenth-century neo-Kantians and institutionalized in nineteenth-century German universities. Carving out a space between ideology and empirical psychology, Germany philosophy wrote its own history, producing our modern canon of the "greats." This task was completed by the end of the nineteenth century. The narrative of the history of philosophy as a series of great thinkers continues today in introductory philosophy courses. Philosophy's claim to intellectual preeminence lasted only for a short time, however, and by the 1920s, only philosophers and undergraduates believed that philosophy was uniquely qualified to ground and judge cultural production. Neither Einstein nor Picasso was overly concerned with what Husserl might have thought of them.

Although philosophy departments continue to teach epistemology, there is a counter-tradition in modern thought that followed another path. Rorty observes, Wittgenstein, Heidegger, and Dewey are in agreement that the notion of knowledge as accurate representation, made possible by special mental processes, and intelligible through a general theory of representation, needs to be abandoned" (6). These thinkers did not seek to construct alternate and better theories of the mind or knowledge. Their aim was not to improve epistemology but to play a different game. Rorty calls this game hermeneutics. By this, he simply means knowledge without foundations; a knowledge that essentially amounts to edifying conversation. Rorty has so far told us very little about the content of this conversation, perhaps because there is very little to tell. As with Wittgenstein, Heidegger, and, in a different way, Dewey, Rorty is faced with the fact, troubling or amusing, that once the historical or logical deconstruction of Western philosophy has been accomplished, there is really nothing special left for philosophers to do. Once it is seen that philosophy does not found or legitimate the claims to knowledge of other disciplines, its task becomes one of commenting on their works and engaging them in conversation.

TRUTH VERSUS TRUTH OR FALSITY

Even if one accepts Rorty's deconstruction of epistemology, the consequences of such a move remain very open. Before exploring some of them, it is important to underline the point that rejecting epistemology does not mean rejecting truth, reason, or standards of judgment. This point is made very succinctly by Ian Hacking in "Language, Truth, and Reason."[2] Hacking puts forward what is basically a simple point: what is currently taken as "truth" is dependent on a prior historical event—the emergence of a style of thinking about truth and falsity that established the conditions for entertaining a proposition as being capable of being taken as true or false in the first place. Hacking puts it this way: "By reasoning I don't mean logic. I mean the very opposite, for logic is the preservation of truth, while a style of reasoning is what brings in the possibility of truth or falsehood . . . styles of reasoning create the possibility of truth and falsehood. Deduction and induction merely preserve it" (56–57). Hacking is not "against" logic, only against its claims to found and ground all truth. Logic is fine in its own domain, but that domain is a limited one.

By drawing this distinction one avoids the problem of totally relativizing reason or of turning different historical conceptions of truth and falsity into a question of subjectivism. These conceptions are historical and social facts. This point is well put by Hacking when he says: "Hence although whichever propositions are truth may depend on the data, the fact that they are candidates for being true is a consequence of an historical event" (56). That the analytical tools we use when we investigate a set of problems— geometry for the Greeks, experimental method in the seventeenth century, or statistics in modern social science—have shifted is explainable without recourse to some truth denying relativism. Furthermore, science understood in this way remains quite objective "simply because the styles of reasoning that we employ determine what counts as objectivity. . . . Propositions of the sort that necessarily require reasoning to be substantiated have a positivity, a being truth or false, only in consequence of the styles of reasoning in which they occur" (49, 65). What Foucault has called the regime, or game, of truth and falsity is both a component and a production of historical practices. Other procedures and other objects could have filled the bill just as well.

Hacking distinguishes between everyday, commonsensical reasoning that does not need to apply any elaborate set of reasons and those more specialized domains that do. There is both a cultural and a historical plurality of these specialized domains and of historically and culturally diverse styles associated with them. From the acceptance of a diversity of historical styles of reasoning, of methods, and objects, Hacking draws the conclusion that thinkers frequently got things right, solved problems, and established truths. But, he argues, this does not imply that we should search for a unified Popperian realm of the true; rather, à la Paul Feyerabend, we should keep our options in inquiry as open as possible. The Greeks, Hacking reminds us, had no concept, or use, of statistics, a fact that invalidates neither Greek science nor statistics as such. This position is not relativism, but it is not imperialism either. Rorty calls his version of all this hermeneutics. Hacking calls his "anarcho-rationalism." Anarcho-rationalism is "tolerance for other people combined with the discipline of one's own standards of truth and reason" (65). Let us call it good thinking.

Michel Foucault has also considered many of these issues in a parallel, but not identical, fashion. His *Archaeology of Knowledge* (1976) is perhaps the most developed attempt to present, if not a theory of what Hacking refers to as "styles of thought," then at least an analytic of them. Several points of Foucault's systematization of how discursive objects, enunciative modalities, concepts, and discursive strategies are formed and transformed are relevant here. Let us merely take one example as illustrative. In the *Discourse on Language* Foucault discusses some of the constraints on, and conditions for, the production of truth, understood as statements capable of being taken seriously as true or false. Among others, Foucault examines the existence of scientific disciplines. He says: "For a discipline to exist, there must be the possibility of formulating—and of doing so *ad infinitum*—fresh propositions. . . . These propositions . . . must fulfill some onerous and complex conditions before they can be admitted within a discipline; before it can be pronounced true or false it must be, as Monsieur Canguilhem might say, 'within the truth.' "[3]

Foucault gives the example of Mendel: "Mendel spoke of objects, employed methods and placed himself within a theoretical perspective totally alien to the biology of his time. . . . Mendel spoke the truth, but he was not *dans le vrai* of contemporary biological discourse" (224). The demonstration of the richness of this style of thinking has been the great strength of Foucault, Georges Canguilhem, and other French practitioners of the history and philosophy of science, particularly the "life sciences."

It is perhaps not accidental that both Rorty and Hacking are concerned with the history of physical science, mathematics, and philosophy. What has been missing from their accounts is the category of power, and to a lesser extent (in Hacking's case) society. Hacking's work on nineteenth-century statistics does, however, include these categories. Although compelling in its deconstructive force, Rorty's story is less convincing in its refusal to comment on how the epistemological turning came about in Western society— according to Rorty, like Galilean science, it just happened—or in its inability to see knowledge as more than free and edifying conversation. Not unlike Jurgen Habermas, although refusing Habermas's striving for foundationalism, Rorty sees free communication, civilized conversation, as the ultimate goal. As Hacking says: "Perhaps Richard Rorty's . . . central doctrine of conversation will some day seem as linguistic a philosophy as the analysis emanating from Oxford a generation ago."[4] The content of the conversation and how the freedom to have it is to come about is, however, beyond the domain of philosophy.

But conversation, between individuals or cultures, is only possible within contexts shaped and constrained by historical, cultural, and political relations and the only partially discursive social practices that constitute them. What is missing from Rorty's account, then, is any discussion of how thought and social practices interconnect. Rorty is helpful in deflating philosophy's claims, but he stops exactly at the point of taking seriously his own insight: to wit, thought is nothing more and nothing less than a historically locatable set of practices. How to do this without reverting to epistemology or to some dubious superstructure/infrastructure device is another question, one Rorty is not alone in not having solved.

REPRESENTATIONS AND SOCIETY

Michel Foucault has offered us some important tools for analyzing thought as a public and social practice. Foucault accepts the main elements of the Nietzschean, Heideggerean account of Western metaphysics and epistemology Rorty has given us, but draws different conclusions from these insights—ones, it seems to me, that are both more consistent and more interesting than Rorty's. We find, for example, many of the same elements that are in Rorty's history of philosophy—the modern subject, representations, order—in Foucault's famous analysis of Velázquez's painting *Las Meninas*. But there are also some major differences. Instead of treating the problem of representations as specific to the history of ideas, Foucault treats it as a more general cultural concern, a problem that was being worked on in many other domains. In *The Order of Things* and later books, Foucault demonstrates how the problem of correct representations has informed a multitude of social domains and practices, ranging from disputes in botany to proposals for prison reform. The problem of representations for Foucault is not, therefore, one that happened to pop up in philosophy and dominate thinking there for three hundred years. It is linked to the wide range of disparate, but interrelated, social and political practices that constitute the modern world, with its distinctive concerns with order, truth, and the subject. Foucault differs from Rorty, then, in treating philosophical ideas as social practices and not chance twists in a conversation or in philosophy.

But Foucault also disagrees with many Marxist thinkers, who see problems in painting as, by definition, ultimately epiphenomenal to, or expressive of, what was "really" going on in society. This brings us briefly to the problem of ideology. In several places, Foucault suggests that once one sees the problem of the subject, or representations, and of truth as social practices, then the very notion of ideology becomes problematic. He says: "behind the concept of ideology there is a kind of nostalgia for a quasi-transparent form of knowledge, free from all error and illusion."[5] In this sense, the concept of ideology is close kin to the concept of epistemology.

For Foucault, the modern concept of ideology is characterized by three interrelated qualities: (1) by definition, ideology is opposed to something like "the truth," a false representation as it were; (2) ideology is produced by a subject (individual or collective) in order to hide the truth, and consequently the analyst's task consists in exposing this false representation; and revealing that (3) ideology is secondary to something more real, some infrastructural dimension on which ideology is parasitic. Foucault rejects all three claims.

We have already alluded to the broad lines of a critique of the subject and the search for certainty seen as based on correct representations. Consequently, let us briefly focus on the third point: the question of whether the production of truth is epiphenomenal to something else. Foucault has described his project not as deciding the truth or falsity of claims in history "but in seeing historically how effects of truth are produced within discourses which in themselves are neither true nor false" (131–33). He proposes to study what he calls the regime of truth as an effective component in the constitution of social practices. He proposes three working hypotheses: "(1) Truth is to be understood as a system of ordered procedures for the production, regulation, distribution, circulation and operation of statements. (2) Truth is linked in a circular relation with systems of power which produce and sustain it, and to effects of power which it induces and which extend it. (3) This regime is not merely ideological or super-structural: it was a condition of the formation and development of capitalism" (133).

As Max Weber once said, seventeenth-century capitalists were not only economic men who traded and built ships, they also looked at Rembrandt's paintings, drew maps of the world, had marked conceptions of the nature of other peoples, and worried a good deal about their own destiny. These representations were strong and effective forces in what they were and how they acted. Many new possibilities for thought and action are opened up if with Rorty we abandon epistemology (or at least see it for what is has been: an important cultural movement in Western society) and follow Foucault in seeing power as productive and permeative of social relations and the production of truth in our current regime of power. Here are some initial conclusions and research strategies that might follow from this discussion of epistemology. I merely list them before moving on to recent discussions in anthropology on how best to describe "the Other."

1. Epistemology must be seen as a historical event—a distinctive social practice, one among many others, articulated in new ways in seventeenth-century Europe.

2. We do not need a theory of indigenous epistemologies or a new epistemology of the Other. We should be attentive to our historical practice of projecting our cultural practices onto the Other; the task is to show how and when and through what cultural and institutional means other people started claiming epistemology for their own.

3. We need to anthropologize the West: show how exotic its constitution of reality has been; emphasize those domains most taken for granted as universal (this includes epistemology and economics); make them seem as historically peculiar as possible; show how their claims to truth are linked to social practices and have hence become effective forces in the social world.

4. We must pluralize and diversify our approaches: a basic move against either economic or philosophic hegemony is to avoid the error of reverse essentializing—Occidentalism is not a remedy for Orientalism.

The Writing of Ethnographic Texts:
The Fantasia of the Library

There is a curious time lag as concepts move across disciplinary boundaries. The moment when the historical profession is discovering cultural anthropology in the (unrepresentative) person of Clifford Geertz is just the moment when Geertz is being questioned in anthropology. So, too, anthropologists, or some of them in any case, are now discovering and being moved to new creation by the infusion of ideas from deconstructionist literary criticism, now that it is losing its cultural energy in literature departments and Derrida is discovering politics. Although there are many carriers of this hybridization there is only one "professional," so to speak, in the anthropological crowd. James Clifford has created and occupied the role of *ex officio* scribe of our scribblings. Geertz, the founding figure, may pause between monographs to muse on texts, narrative, description, and interpretation. Clifford takes as his natives, as well as his informants, those anthropologists past and present whose work, self-consciously or not, has been the production of texts, the writing of ethnography. We are being observed and inscribed.

At first glance James Clifford's work seems to follow naturally in the wake of Geertz's interpretive turn. There is, however, a major difference. Geertz is still directing his efforts to reinvent an anthropological science with the help of textual mediations. The core activity is still social description of the Other, however modified by new conceptions of discourse, author, or text. The other for Clifford is the anthropological representation of the other. This means that Clifford is simultaneously more firmly in control of his project and more parasitical. He can invent his questions with few constraints; he must constantly feed off others' texts.

This new specialty is currently in the process of self-definition. The first move in legitimating a new approach is to claim it has an object of study, preferably an important one, that has previously escaped notice. Parallel to Geertz's claim that the Balinese were interpreting their cockfights as cultural texts all along, Clifford argues that anthropologists have been experimenting with writing

37

forms whether they knew it or not. The interpretive turn in anthropology has made its mark (producing a substantial body of work and almost establishing itself as a subspecialty), but it is still not clear whether the deconstructive-semiotic turn (an admittedly vague label) is a salutary loosening up, an opening for exciting new work of major import, or a tactic in the field of cultural politics to be understood primarily in sociological terms. As it is certainly the first and the third, it is worth a closer examination.

In his essay "Fantasia of the Library,"[6] Michel Foucault plays adroitly with the progression of uses Flaubert made throughout his life of the fable of the temptation of Saint Anthony. Far from being the idle products of a fertile imagination, Flaubert's references to iconography and philology in his seemingly phantasmagoric renderings of the saint's hallucinations were exact ones. Foucault shows us how Flaubert returned throughout his life to this staging of experience and writing, and used it as an ascetic exercise both to produce and to keep at bay the demons that haunt a writer's world. It was no accident that Flaubert ended his life as a writer with that monstrous collection of commonplaces *Bouvard et Pecuchet*. A constant commentary on other texts, *Bouvard et Pecuchet* can be read as a thorough domestication of textuality into a self-contained exercise of arranging and cataloguing—the fantasia of the library.

For the sake of argument, let us juxtapose Clifford Geertz's interpretive anthropology to James Clifford's textualist meta-anthropology. If Geertz is still seeking to conjure and capture the demons of exoticism—theater states, shadow plays, cockfights—through his limited use of fictionalized stagings in which they can appear to us, the textualist/deconstructive move runs the risk of inventing ever more clever filing systems for others' texts and of imagining that everyone else in the world is hard at work doing the same thing. I should stress that I am not saying that Clifford's enterprise has up to the present been anything but salutary. The raising of anthropological consciousness about anthropology's own textual mode of operation was long overdue. Despite Geertz's occasional acknowledgments of the ineluctability of fictionalizing, he has never pushed that insight very far. The point seems to have needed a metaposition to bring home its real force. The voice from the campus library has been a salutary one. What I want to do briefly in this section is to return the gaze, to look back at this ethnographer of ethnographers, sitting across the table in a cafe, and, using his own descriptive categories, examine his textual productions.

Clifford's central theme has been the textual construction of anthropological authority. The main literary device employed in ethnographies, "free indirect style," has been well analyzed by Dan Sperber and need not be rehearsed here.[7] The insight that anthropologists write employing literary conventions, although interesting, is not inherently crisis-provoking. Many now hold that fiction and science are not opposed but complementary terms.[8] Advances have been made in our awareness of the fictional (in the sense of "made," "fabricated") quality of anthropological writing and in the integration of its characteristic modes of production. The self-consciousness of style, rhetoric, and dialectic in the production of anthropological texts should lead us to a finer awareness of other, more imaginative, ways to write.

Clifford seems, however, to be saying more than this. Substantively, he argues that from Malinowski on, anthropological authority has rested on two textual legs. An experiential "I was there" element establishes the unique authority of the anthropologist; its suppression in the text establishes the anthropologist's scientific authority. Clifford shows us this device at work in Geertz's famous cockfight paper: "The research process is separated from the texts it generates and from the fictive world they are made to call up. The actuality of discursive situations and individual interlocutors is filtered out. . . . The dialogical, situational aspects of ethnographic interpretation tend to be banished from the final representative text. Not entirely banished, of course; there exist approved *topoi* for the portrayal of the research process."[9] Clifford presents Geertz's "appealing fable" as paradigmatic: the anthropologist establishes that he was there and then disappears from the text.

With his own genre Clifford makes a parallel move. Just as Geertz makes a bow to self-referentiality (thereby establishing one

39

dimension of his authority) and then (in the name of science) evades its consequences, so, too, Clifford talks a great deal about the ineluctability of dialogue (thereby establishing his authority as an "open" one), but his texts are not themselves dialogic. They are written in a modified free indirect style. They evoke an "I was there at the anthropology convention" tone, while consistently maintaining a Flaubertean remove. Both Geertz and Clifford fail to use self-referentiality as anything more than a device for establishing authority. Clifford's telling reading of the Balinese cockfight as a panoptic construct makes this point persuasively, but he himself makes the same omission on another level. He reads and classifies, describing intention and establishing a canon; but his own writing and situation are left unexamined. Pointing out Clifford's textual stance does not, of course, invalidate his insights (anymore than his reading of Malinowski's textual moves invalidates the analysis of the Kula). It only situates them. We have moved back from the tent in the Trobriands filled with natives to the writing desk in the campus library.

An essential move in establishing disciplinary or subdisciplinary legitimacy is classification. Clifford proposed four types of anthropological writing, which have appeared in roughly chronological order. He organizes his essay "On Ethnographic Authority" around this progression but also asserts that no mode of authority is better than any other. "The modes of authority reviewed in this essay—experiential, interpretive, dialogical, polyphonic—are available to all writers of ethnographic texts, Western and non-Western. None is obsolete, none is pure: there is room for invention within each paradigm" (142). This conclusion goes against the rhetorical grain of Clifford's essay. This tension is important and I shall return to it below.

Clifford's main thesis is that anthropological writing has tended to suppress the dialogic dimension of fieldwork, giving full control of the text to the anthropologist. The bulk of Clifford's work has been devoted to showing ways in which this textual elimination of the dialogical might be remedied by new forms of writing. This leads him to read experiential and interpretive modes of writing as monological, linked in general terms to colonialism.

"Interpretive anthropology . . . in its mainstream realist strands . . . does not escape the general strictures of those critics of 'colonial' representation who, since 1950, have rejected discourses that portray the cultural realities of other people without placing their own reality in jeopardy" (133). It would be easy to read this statement as preferring some "paradigms" to others. It is perfectly possible that Clifford himself is simply ambivalent. However, given his own interpretive choices he clearly does characterize some modes as "emergent" and thereby as temporarily more important. Using a grid of interpretation that highlights the suppression of the dialogic, it is hard not to read the history of anthropological writing as a loose progression toward dialogical and polyphonic textuality.

Having cast the first two modes of ethnographic authority (experiential and realist/interpretive) in largely negative terms, Clifford moves on to a much more enthusiastic portrayal of the next set (dialogic and heteroglossic). He says: "Dialogic and constructivist paradigms tend to disperse or share out ethnographic authority, while narratives of initiation confirm the researcher's special competence. Paradigms of experience and interpretation are yielding to paradigms of discourse, of dialogue and polyphony" (133). The claim that such modes are triumphing is empirically dubious; as Renato Rosaldo says: "The troops are not following." Yet there is clearly considerable interest in such matters.

What is dialogic? Clifford at first seems to be using the term in a literal sense: a text that presents two subjects in discursive exchange. Kevin Dwyer's "rather literal record" (134) of exchanges with a Moroccan farmer is the first example cited of a "dialogic" text. However, a page later, Clifford adds: "To say that an ethnography is composed of discourses and that its different components are dialogically related, is not to say that its textual form should be that of a literal dialogue" (135). Alternate descriptions are given, but no final definition is arrived at. Consequently the genre's defining characteristics remain unclear. "But if interpretive authority is based on the exclusion of dialogue, the reverse is also true: a purely dialogical authority represses the inescapable fact of textualization," Clifford quickly moves on to remind us (134). This is

41

confirmed by Dwyer's adamant distancing of himself from what he perceives as textualist trends in anthropology. The opposition of interpretive and dialogic is hard to grasp—several pages later Clifford praises the most renowned representative of hermeneutics, Hans Georg Gadamer, whose texts certainly contain no direct dialogues, for aspiring to "radical dialogism" (142). Finally, Clifford asserts that dialogic texts are, after all, texts, merely "representations" of dialogues. The anthropologist retains his or her authority as a constitution subject and representative of the dominant culture. Dialogic texts can be just as staged and controlled as experiential or interpretive texts. The mode offers no textual guarantees.

Finally, beyond dialogic texts, lies heteroglossia: "a carnivalesque arena of diversity." Following Mikhail Bakhtin, Clifford points to Dickens's work as an example of the "polyphonic space" that might serve as a model for us. "Dickens, the actor, oral performer, and the polyphonist, is set against Flaubert, the master of authorial control moving Godlike, among the thoughts and feelings of his characters. Ethnography, like the novel, wrestles with these alternatives" (137). If dialogic texts fall prey to the evils of totalizing ethnographic adjustment, then perhaps even more radical heteroglossic ones might not: "Ethnography is invaded by heteroglossia. If accorded an autonomous textual space, transcribed at a sufficient length, indigenous statements make sense on terms different from those of the arranging ethnographer. . . . This suggests an alternate textual strategy, a utopia of plural authorship that accords to collaborators, not merely the status of independent enunciators, but that of writers" (140).

But Clifford immediately adds: "quotations are always staged by the quoter . . . a more radical polyphony would only displace ethnographic authority, still confirming, the final, virtuoso orchestration by a single author of all the discourses in his or her text" (139). New forms of writing, new textual experiments would open new possibilities—but guarantee none. Clifford is uneasy about this. He moves on. Temporarily enthusiastic for dialogic, Clifford immediately qualifies his praise. He leads us on to heteroglossia: seduced—for a paragraph—until we see that it too is, alas, writing.

Clifford closes his essay by proclaiming: "I have argued that this imposition of coherence on an unruly textual process is now, inescapably, a matter of strategic choice" (142).

Clifford's presentation clearly offers a progression even if, by the end of the essay, it is a purely decisionist one. However, Clifford explicitly denies any hierarchy. At first I thought this was mere inconsistency, or ambivalence, or the embodiment of an unresolved but creative tension. I now think that Clifford, like everyone else, is "*dans le vrai.*" We are at a discursive moment in which the author's intentions have been eliminated or underplayed in recent critical thought. Rather, we have been led to question the structures and contours of various modes of writing per se.

FROM MODERNISM TO POST-MODERNISM IN ANTHROPOLOGY

Fredric Jameson, in his "Postmodernism and Consumer Society," offers us some useful starting points to situate recent developments in anthropological and meta-anthropological writing.[10] Without seeking a univocal definition of post-modernism, Jameson delimits the scope of the term by proposing a number of key elements: its historical location, its use of pastiche, the importance of images.

Jameson locates post-modernism culturally and historically not just as a stylistic term but as a period marker. By so doing he seeks to isolate and correlate features of cultural production in the 1960s with other social and economic transformations. The establishment of analytic criteria and their correlation with socio-economic changes is very preliminary in Jameson's account, little more than a place marker. However, it is worth marking the place. Late capitalism is defined by Jameson as the moment when "the last vestiges of Nature which survived on into classical capitalism are at last eliminated: namely the third world and the unconscious. The 60s will then have been the momentous transformational period in which this systemic restructuring takes place on a global scale" (207). Jameson's provisional periodization gives us the possibility of discussing changes in representational forms.

The various post-modernisms forming in the sixties surfaced, at least in part, as a reaction against the earlier modernist movements. Classical modernism, to use an expression that is no longer oxymoronic, arose in the context of high capitalist and bourgeois society and stood against it: "it emerged within the business society of the gilded age as scandalous and offensive to the middle class public—ugly, dissonant, sexually shocking . . . subversive" (124). Jameson contrasts the subversive modernist turn of the early twentieth century with the flattening, reactive nature of post-modern culture. Those formerly subversive and embattled styles—Abstract Expressionism; the great modernist poetry of Pound, Eliot, or Wallace Stevens; the International Style (Le Corbusier, Frank Lloyd Wright, Mies); Stravinsky; Joyce, Proust, and Mann—felt to be scandalous or shocking by our grandparents are, for the generation which arrives at the gate in the 1960s, felt to be the establishment and the enemy—dead, stifling, canonical, the reified monuments one has to destroy to do anything new. This means that there will be as many different forms of post-modernism as there were high modernism in place, since the former are at least initially specific and local reactions against those models (111–12).[11]

I would add that if post-modernism arose in the 1960s in part as a reaction to the academic canonization of the great modernist artists, it has itself succeeded in entering the academy in the 1980s. It has successfully domesticated and packaged itself through the proliferation of classificatory schemes, the construction of canons, the establishment of hierarchies, blunting of offensive behavior, acquiescence to university norms. Just as there are now art galleries for graffiti in New York, so, too, there are theses being written on graffiti, break dancing, and so on, in the most avant-garde departments.

What is post-modernism? The first element is its historical location as a counter-reaction to modernism. Going beyond the by now "classic" definition of Lyotard—the end of metanarratives—Jameson defines its second element as pastiche. The dictionary definition—"(1) An artistic composition drawn from several sources, (2) a hodge podge"—is not sufficient. Pound, for example, drew from several sources. Jameson is pointing at a use of pastiche that has lost its normative moorings, which sees the jumbling of elements as all there is. Hodge podge is defined as "a jumbled mixture," but it comes from the French *hochepot*, a stew, and therein lies the difference.

Joyce, Hemingway, Woolf, et al., began with the conceit of an interiorized and distinctive subjectivity that both drew from and stood at a distance from normal speech and identity. There was "a linguistic norm in contrast to which the styles of the great modernists"[12] could be attacked or praised, but in either case gauged. But what if this tension between bourgeois normality and the modernists' stylistic limit testing cracked, yielding to a social reality in which we had nothing but "stylistic diversity and heterogeneity" without the assumption (however contestable) of relatively stable identity or linguistic norms? Under such conditions, the contestatory stance of the modernists would lose its force: "all that is left is to imitate dead styles, to speak through the masks and with the voices of the styles in the imaginary museum. But this means that contemporary or post-modernist art is going to be about art itself in a new kind of way, even more, it means that one of its essential messages will involve the necessary failure of art and the aesthetic, the failure of the new, the imprisonment in the past" (15 16). It seems to me that this imprisonment in the past is quite different from historicism. Post-modernism moves beyond the (what now seems to be almost comforting) estrangement of historicism, which looked, from a distance, at other cultures as wholes. The dialectic of Self and Other may have produced an alienated relationship, but it was one with definable norms, identities, and relations. Today, beyond estrangement and relativism, lies pastiche.

To exemplify this, Jameson develops an analysis of nostalgia films. Contemporary nostalgia films such as *Chinatown* or *Body Heat* are characterized by a "retrospective styling," dubbed *la mode retro* by French critics. As opposed to traditional historical films which seek to re-create the fiction of another age as other, *mode retro* films seeks to evoke a feeling tone through the use of precise artifacts and stylistic devices that blur temporal boundaries. Jameson points out that recent nostalgia films often take place in the present (or, as in the case of *Star Wars*, in the future). A proliferation of meta-references to other representations flattens and empties their contents. One of their chief devices is to draw heavily on older plots: "The allusive and elusive plagiarism of older plots is, of course, also a feature of pastiche" (117). These films function not so much to deny the present but to blur the specificity of the past, to confuse the line between past and present (or future) as distinct periods. What these films do is represent our representations of other eras. "If there is any realism left here, it is a 'realism' which springs from the shock of grasping that confinement and of realizing that, for whatever peculiar reasons, we seem condemned to seek the historical past through our own pop images and stereotypes about that past, which itself remains forever out of reach" (118). This, it seems to me, describes an approach that sees strategic choice of representations of representations as its main problem.

Although Jameson is writing about historical consciousness, the same trend is present in ethnographic writing: interpretive anthropologists work with the problem of representations of others' representations, historians and metacritics of anthropology with the classification, canonization, and "making available" of representations of representation of representations. The historical flattening found in the pastiche of nostalgia films reappears in the meta-ethnographic flattening that makes all the world's cultures practitioners of textuality. The details in these narratives are precise, the images evocative, the neutrality exemplary, and the mode *retro*.

The final feature of post-modernism for Jameson is "textuality." Drawing on Lacanian ideas about schizophrenia, Jameson points to one of the defining characteristics of the textual movement as the breakdown of the relationship between signifiers: "schizophrenia is an experience of isolated, disconnected, discontinuous material signifiers which fail to link up into a coherent

46

sequence . . . a signifier that has lost its signified has thereby been transformed into an image" (120). Although the use of the term schizophrenic obscures more than it illuminates, the point is telling. Once the signifier is freed from a concern with its relation to an external referent it does not float free of any referentiality at all; rather, its reference becomes other texts, other images. For Jameson, post-modern texts (he is talking about Language poets) parallel this move: "Their references are other images, another text, and the unity of the poem is not in the text at all but outside it in the bound unity of an absent book" (123). We are back at the "Fantasia of the Library," this time not as bitter parody but as celebratory pastiche.

Obviously this does not mean that we can solve the current crisis of representation by fiat. A return to earlier modes of unselfconscious representation is not a coherent position (although the news has not yet arrived in most anthropology departments). But we cannot solve it by ignoring the relations of representational forms and social practices either. If we attempt to eliminate social referentiality, other referents will occupy the voided position. Thus the reply of Dwyer's Moroccan informant (when asked which part of their dialogue has interested him most) that he had not been interested in a single question asked by Dwyer is not troubling as long as other anthropologists read the book and include it in their discourse. But obviously neither Dwyer nor Clifford would be satisfied with that response. Their intentions and their discourse strategies diverge. It is the latter that seem to have gone astray.

INTERPRETIVE COMMUNITIES, POWER RELATIONS, ETHICS

> The young conservatives . . . claim as their own
> the revelations of a decentering subjectivity,
> emancipated from the imperatives of work and
> usefulness, and with this experience they step
> outside the modern world. . . . They remove

47

into the sphere of the Far-away and the archaic
the spontaneous powers of imagination,
self-experience and emotion.
(Jurgen Habermas, "Modernity—
An Incomplete Project")

A variety of important writing in the past decades has explored the historical relations between world macropolitics and anthropology: The West vs. The Rest; Imperialism; Colonialism: Neo-Colonialism. Work ranging from Talal Asad on colonialism and anthropology to Edward Said on Western discourse and the Other have put these questions squarely on the agenda of contemporary debate. However, as Talal Asad has pointed out, this by no means implies that these macropolitical economic conditions have been significantly affected by what goes on in anthropological debates. We also now know a good deal about the relations of power and discourse that obtain between the anthropologist and the people with whom "he/she" works. Both the macro- and microrelations of power and discourse between anthropology and its Other are at last open to inquiry. We know some of the questions worth asking and have made asking them part of the discipline's agenda.

The metareflections on the crisis of representation in ethnographic writing indicate a shift away from concentrating on relations with other cultures to a (nonthematized) concern with traditions of representation, and metatraditions of metarepresentations, in our culture. I have been using Clifford's metaposition as a touchstone. He is not talking primarily about relations with the Other, except as mediated through his central analytic concern, discursive tropes, and strategies. This has taught us important things. I have claimed, however, that this approach contains an interesting blind spot, a refusal of self-reflection. Fredric Jameson's analysis of post-modern culture was introduced as a kind of anthropological perspective on this cultural development. Jameson suggests ways of thinking about the appearance of this new crisis of representation as a historical event with its own specific historical constraints. He enables us to see that in important ways not shared by other critical stances (which have their own characteristic blind spots) the post-modernist is blind to her own situation and situatedness because, qua post-modernist, she is committed to a doctrine of partiality and flux for which even such things as one's own situation are so unstable, so without identity, that they cannot serve as objects of sustained reflection. Postmodern pastiche is both a critical position and a dimension of our contemporary world. Jameson's analysis helps us to establish an understanding of their interconnections, thereby avoiding both nostalgia and the mistake of universalizing or ontologizing a very particular historical situation.

In my opinion, the stakes in recent debates about writing are not directly political in the conventional sense of the term. I have argued elsewhere that the politics involved is academic politics, and that this level of politics has not been explored.[13] The work of Pierre Bourdieu is helpful in posing questions about the politics of culture.[14] Bourdieu has taught us to ask in what field of power, and from what position in that field, any given author writes. His sociology of cultural production does not seek to reduce knowledge to social position or interest per se but, rather, to place all of these variables within the complex constraints—Bourdieu's *habitus*—within which they are produced and received. Bourdieu is particularly attentive to strategies of cultural power that advance through denying their attachment to immediate political ends and thereby accumulate both symbolic capital and "high" structural position.

Bourdieu's work would lead us to suspect that contemporary academic proclamations of anti-colonialism, while admirable, are not the whole story. These proclamations must be seen as political moves within the academic community. Neither Clifford nor any of the rest of us is writing in the late 1950s. His audiences are neither colonial officers nor those working under the aegis of colonial power. Our political field is more familiar: the academy in the 1980s. Hence, though not exactly false, situating the crisis of representation within the context of the rupture of decolonization is, given the way it is handled, basically beside the point. It is true to the extent that anthropology is certainly reflective of the course of larger world events, and specifically of changing historical relations with the groups it studies. Asserting that new ethnographic writing emerged because of decolonization, however, leaves out precisely those mediations that would make historical sense of the present object of study.

One is led to consider the politics of interpretation in the academy today. Asking whether longer, dispersive, multi-authored texts would yield tenure might seem petty. But those are the dimensions of power relations to which Nietzsche exhorted us to be scrupulously attentive. There can be no doubt of the existence and influence of this type of power relation in the production of texts. We owe these less glamorous, if more immediately constraining, conditions more attention. The taboo against specifying them is much greater than the strictures against denouncing colonialism; an anthropology of anthropology would include them. Just as there was formerly a discursive knot preventing discussion of exactly those fieldwork practices that defined the authority of the anthropologist, which has now been untied, so, too, the micropractices of the academy might well do with some scrutiny.

Another way of posing this problem is to refer to "corridor talk." For many years, anthropologists informally discussed fieldwork experiences among themselves. Gossip about an anthropologist's field experiences was an important component of that person's reputation. But such matters were not, until recently, written about "seriously." It remains in the corridors and faculty clubs. But what cannot be publicly discussed cannot be analyzed or rebutted. Those domains that cannot be analyzed or refuted, and yet are directly central to hierarchy, should not be regarded as innocent or irrelevant. We know that one of the most common tactics of an elite group is to refuse to discuss—to label as vulgar or uninteresting—issues that are uncomfortable for them. When corridor talk about fieldwork becomes discourse we learn a good deal. Moving the conditions of production of anthropological knowledge out of the domain of gossip—where it remains the property of those around to hear it—into that of knowledge would be a step in the right direction.

My wager is that looking at the conditions under which people are hired, given tenure, published, awarded grants, and feted would repay the effort. How has the "deconstructionist" wave differed from the other major trend in the academy in the past decade—feminism? How are the careers made and destroyed now? What are the boundaries of taste? Who established and who enforces these civilities? Whatever else we know, we certainly know that the material conditions under which the textual movement has flourished must include the university, its micropolitics, its trends. We know that this level of power relations effects us, influences our themes, forms, contents, audiences. We owe these issues attention—if only to establish their relative weight. Then, as with fieldwork, we shall be able to proceed.[15]

STOP MAKING SENSE: DIALOGUE AND IDENTITY

Marilyn Strathern, in a challenging paper, "Dislodging a World View: Challenge and Counter-Challenge in the Relationship between Feminism and Anthropology," has taken an important step in situating the strategy of recent textualist writing through a comparison with recent work by anthropological feminists.[16] Strathern makes a distinction between feminist anthropology, an anthropological subdiscipline contributing to the discipline's advancement, and an anthropological feminism whose aim is to build a feminist community, one whose premises and goals differ from, and are opposed to, anthropology. In the latter enterprise, difference and conflict—as historical conditions of identity and knowledge—are the valorized terms, not science and harmony.

Strathern reflects on her annoyance when a senior male colleague praised feminist anthropology for enriching the discipline. He said: "Let a thousand flowers bloom." She says: "Indeed it is true in general that feminist critique has enriched anthropology—opened up new understandings of ideology, the construction of symbolic systems, resources management, property concepts, and so on." Anthropology, in its relative openness and eclecticism, has integrated these scientific advances, at first reluctantly, now eagerly. Strathern, drawing on Kuhn's much-used paradigm concept, points out that this is how normal science works.

Yet the "let a thousand flowers bloom" tolerance produced a sense of unease; later, Strathern realized that her unease stemmed from a sense that feminists should be laboring in other fields, not adding flowers to anthropology's.

Strathern distances her own practice from the normal science model in two ways. First, she claims that social and natural science are different: "not simply [because] within any one discipline one finds diverse 'schools' (also true in science) but that their premises are constructed competitively in relation to one another." Second, this competition does not turn on epistemological issues alone, but ultimately on political and ethical differences. In his essay, "What Makes an Interpretation Acceptable?," Stanley Fish makes a similar point (albeit to advance a very different agenda).[17] He argues that all statements are interpretations, and that all appeals to the text, or the facts, are themselves based on interpretations; these interpretations are community affairs and not subjective (or individual) ones—that is, meanings are cultural or socially available, they are not invented *ex nihilo* by a single interpreter. Finally, all interpretations, most especially those that deny their status as interpretations, are only possible on the basis of other interpretations, whose rules they affirm while announcing their negation.

Fish argues that we never resolve disagreements by an appeal to the facts or the text because "the facts emerge only in the context of some point of view. It follows, then, that disagreements must occur between those who hold (or are held by) different points of view, and what is at stake in a disagreement is the right to specify what the facts can hereafter be said to be. Disagreements are not settled by the facts but are the means by which the facts are settled" (338). Strathern adroitly demonstrates these points in her contrast of anthropological feminism and experimental anthropologists.

The guiding value of those interested in experimental ethnographic writing, Strathern argues, is dialogic: "the effort is to create a relation with the Other—as in the search for a medium of expression which will offer mutual interpretation, perhaps visualized as a common text, or as something more like a discourse." Feminism, for Strathern, proceeds from the initial and unassimilable fact of domination. The attempt to incorporate feminist understandings into an improved science of anthropology or a new rhetoric of dialogue is taken as a further act of violence. Feminist anthropology is trying to shift discourse, not improve a paradigm: "that is, it alters the nature of the audience, the range of readership and the kinds of interactions between author and reader, and alters the subject matter of conversation in the way it allows others to speak—what is talked about and whom one is talking to." Strathern is not seeking to invent a new synthesis, but to strengthen difference.

The ironies here are exhilarating. Experimentalists (almost all male) are nurturing and optimistic, if just a touch sentimental. Clifford claims to be working from a combination of sixties idealism and eighties irony. Textual radicals seek to work toward establishing relationship, to demonstrate the importance of connection and openness, to advance the possibilities of sharing and mutual understanding, while being fuzzy about power and the realities of socioeconomic constraints. Strathern's anthropological feminist insists upon not losing sight of fundamental differences, power relationships, hierarchical domination. She seeks to articulate a communal identity on the basis of conflict, separation, and antagonism: partially as a defense against the threat of encompassment by a paradigm of love, mutuality, and understanding in which she sees other motives and structures, partially as a device to preserve meaningful difference per se as a distinctive value.

Difference is played out on two levels: between feminists and anthropology and within the feminist community. Facing outward, resistance and nonassimilation are the highest values. Within this new interpretive community, however, the virtues of dialogic relationships have been affirmed. Internally, feminists may disagree and compete; but they do so in relation to one another. "It is precisely because feminist theory does not constitute its past as a 'text' that it cannot be added on or supplant anthropology in any simple way. For if feminists always maintain a divide against the Other, among themselves by contrast they create something indeed much closer to discourse than to text. And the character of this discourse approaches the 'interlocutionary common product' for which the new ethnography aims." What tropes are available for all to use, how they are used makes all the difference.

ETHICS AND MODERNITY: REPRESENTATIONS ARE SOCIAL FACTS

> The emergence of factions within a once inter-
> dicted activity is a sure sign of its having achieved
> the status of an orthodoxy.
> *(Stanley Fish, "What Makes an Interpretation Accept-
> able?")*

Recent discussions on the making of ethnographic texts have re-vealed differences and points of opposition as well as important areas of consensus. To borrow yet another of Geertz's phrases, we can, and have been, vexing each other with profit, the touchstone of interpretive advance. In this last section, through the device of a schematic juxtaposition of the three positions previously out-lined, I shall propose my own. Although critical of dimensions of each of these positions, I consider them to be parts, if not of an interpretive community, at least of an interpretive federation to which I belong.

Anthropologists, critics, feminists, and critical intellectuals are all concerned with questions of truth and its social location; imag-ination and formal problems of representation; domination and resistance; the ethical subject and techniques for becoming one. These topics are, however, interpreted in differing fashions; dif-ferent dangers and different possibilities are picked out; and dif-ferent hierarchies between these categories are defended.

1. *Interpretive anthropologist.* Truth and science conceived as interpretive practices are the commanding terms. Both anthro-pologist and native are seen as engaged in interpreting the mean-ing of everyday life. Problems of representation are central for both, and are the loci of cultural imagination. Representations are not, however, *sui generis*; they serve as means for making sense of life worlds (which they are instrumental in constructing) and

54

consequently they differ in their functions. The goals of the anthropologists and the native are distinct. To take one example, science and religion differ as cultural systems in strategy, ethos, and ends. The political and ethical positions are important, if largely implicit, anchors. Conceptually, scientific specification concerning cultural difference is at the heart of the project. The greatest danger, seen from the inside, is the confusion of science and politics. The greatest weakness, seen from the outside, is the historical, political, and experiential *cordon sanitaire* drawn around interpretive science.

2. *Critics.* The guiding principle is formal. The text is primary. Attentiveness to the tropes and rhetorical devices through which authority is constructed allows the introduction of themes of domination, exclusion, and inequality as subject matter. But they are only material. They are given form by the critic/writer, be she anthropologist or native: "Other Tribes, Other Scribes." We change ourselves primarily through imaginative constructions. The kind of beings we want to become are open, permeable ones, suspicious of metanarratives; pluralizers. But authorial control seems to blunt self-reflection and the dialogic impulse. The danger: the obliteration of meaningful difference, Weber's museumification of the world. The truth that experience and meaning are mediated representationally can be over-extended to equate experience and meaning with the formal dimension of representation.

3. *Political subjects.* The guiding value is the constitution of a community-based political subjectivity. Anthropological feminists work against an Other cast as essentially different and violent. Within the community the search for truth, as well as social and aesthetic experimentation are guided by a dialogic desire. The fictive other allows a pluralizing set of differences to appear. The risk is that these enabling fictions of essential difference may become reified, thereby reduplicating the oppressive social forms they were meant to undermine. Strathern puts this point well: "Now if feminism mocks the anthropological pretension of creating a product in some ways jointly authored then anthropology mocks the pretension that feminists can ever really achieve the separation they desire."

4. *Cosmopolitan intellectuals.* I have emphasized the dangers of high interpretive science and the overly sovereign represented, and am excluded from direct participation in the feminist dialogue. Let me propose a critical cosmopolitanism as a fourth figure. The ethical is the guiding value. This is an oppositional position, one suspicious of sovereign powers, universal truths, overly relativized preciousness, local authenticity, moralisms high and low. Understanding is its second value, but an understanding suspicious of its own imperial tendencies. It attempts to be highly attentive to (and respectful of) difference, but is also wary of the tendency to essentialize difference. What we share as a condition of existence, heightened today by our ability, and at times our eagerness, to obliterate one another, is a specificity of historical experience and place, however complex and contestable they might be, and a worldwide macro-interdependency encompassing any local particularity. Whether we like it or not, we are all in this situation. Borrowing a term applied during different epochs to Christians, aristocrats, merchants, Jews, homosexuals, and intellectuals (while changing its meaning), I call the acceptance of this twin valorization *cosmopolitanism.* Let us define cosmopolitanism as an ethos of macro-interdependencies, with an acute consciousness (often forced upon people) of the inescapabilities and particularities of places, characters, historical trajectories, and fates. *Homo sapiens* has done rather poorly in interpreting this condition. We seem to have trouble with the balancing act, preferring to reify local identities or construct universal ones. We live in between. The Sophists offer a fictive figure for this slot: eminently Greek, yet often excluded from citizenship in the various *poleis;* cosmopolitan insider's outsiders of a particular historical and cultural world; not members of a projected universal regime (under God, the imperium, or the laws of reason); devotees of rhetoric and thereby fully aware of its abuses; concerned with the events of the day, but buffered by ironic reserve.

This essay has outlined some of the elements and forms of contemporary practices of representation. Where these practices lead is unclear. In closing, I simply mark a space for further exploration.

NOTES

1. Richard Rorty, *Philosophy and the Mirror of Nature* (Princeton, N.J.: Princeton University Press, 1979).

2. Ian Hacking, "Language, Truth, and Reason," in *Rationality and Relativism*, ed. R. Hollis and S. Lukes (Cambridge, Mass.: MIT Press, 1982), pp. 185–203.

3. Michel Foucault, "The Discourse on Language," in *The Archaeology of Knowledge* (New York: Harper and Row, 1976), pp. 223–24.

4. Ian Hacking, "Five Parables," in *Philosophy in History*, ed. Richard Rorty, J. B. Scheewind, and Quentin Skinner (Cambridge, U.K.: Cambridge University Press, 1984), pp. 103–24.

5. Michel Foucault, "Truth and Power," in *Power/Knowledge* (New York: Pantheon Books, 1980), pp. 109–33.

6. Michel Foucault, "Fantasia of the Library," in *Language, Counter-Memory, Practice*, ed. Donald Bouchard (Ithaca, N.Y.: Cornell University Press, 1977), pp. 87–109.

7. Dan Sperber, "Ethnographie interprétative et anthropologie théorique," in *Le Savoir des anthropologues* (Paris: Hermann, 1982), pp. 13–48.

8. Michael de Certeau, "History: Ethics, Science, and Fiction," in *Social Science as Moral Inquiry*, ed. Norma Hahn, Robert Bellah, Paul Rabinow, and William Sullivan (New York: Columbia University Press, 1983), pp. 173–209.

9. James Clifford, "On Ethnographic Authority," *Representations* 1, no. 2 (1983): 132.

10. Fredric Jameson, "Postmodernism and Consumer Society," in *The Anti-Aesthetic: Essays on Postmodern Culture*, ed. Hal Foster (Port Townsend, Wash.: Bay Press, 1983), pp. 111–25.

11. Jameson, not unlike Habermas ("Modernity—An Incomplete Project,"in *The Anti-Aesthetic*, 3–15), clearly thinks there were important critical elements in modernism. Although they would probably differ on what they were, they would agree that in an important sense the project of modernity is unfinished, and certain of its features (its attempt to be critical, secular, anti-capitalist, rational) are worth strengthening.

12. Jameson, "Postmodernism and Consumer Society," p. 114.

13. Paul Rabinow, "Discourse and Power: On the Limits of Ethnographic Texts," *Dialectical Anthropology* 10 (1985): 1–13.

14. Pierre Bourdieu, *Distinction* (Cambridge, Mass.: Harvard University Press, 1984); *Homo Academicus* (Paris: Editions de Minuit, 1984).

15. Martin Finkelstein presents a valuable summary of some of these issues in *The American Academic Profession: A Synthesis of Social Scientific Inquiry since World War II* (Columbus, Ohio: Ohio State University Press, 1984).

16. Marilyn Strathern, "Dislodging a World View: Challenge and Counter-Challenge in the Relationship between Feminism and Anthropology," in *Chang-*

ing Paradigms: The Impact of Feminist Theory upon the World of Scholarship, ed. Susan Magarey (Sydney: Hale and Iremonger, 1984).

17. Stanley Fish, "What Makes an Interpretation Acceptable?" In *Is There a Text in This Class?* (Cambridge, Mass.: Harvard University Press, 1980).

CHAPTER 3

On the Archaeology of Late Modernity

PLANNING has at least two archaeological moments, one of which I call techno-cosmopolitanism and the other middling modernism. They are both modern in that they proceed under the imperatives of social modernity—industrialization, bureaucracy, and welfare. Techno-cosmopolitanism shares with other modern projects an understanding that society must be constructed, planned, and organized through art and science. It seeks this end through the use of already existing cultural, social, and aesthetic institutions and spaces seen to embody a healthy sediment of historical practices which need reorganization. Techno-cosmopolitanism is the operationalization of history, society, and culture. It is technological in that the operations are scientifically arrived at and can be specified; it is cosmopolitan in that these technological operations themselves are applied to specific customs, cultures, countries. Thus, while the principles of urban planning in Morocco or Brazil are the same, the well-planned city in Morocco will by necessity differ from one in Brazil in accordance with the specificities of the histories, topographies, cultures, and politics of these places. The art of urban planning and of a healthy modern society lies precisely in the orchestration of the general and the particular.[1]

Middling modernism shares the norms of industrialization, health, and sociality as well as the technological processes aimed at operationalizing social practices. However, the material it operates on is no longer the sedimented historical and cultural practices of a particular society which it seeks to bring into modernity; rather, the "human material," to use a telling phrase of Maurice Halbwachs, on which it works is a universal subject whose needs, potentialities, and norms can be discovered by science. Techno-cosmopolitanism claimed that health, productivity, and efficiency (an orderly modern society) could be achieved only through a

59

reordering and reactivation of essentially healthy sedimented practices—society depended on history. Middling modernism's project was more audacious, seeking to create New Men freed, purified, and liberated to pursue new forms of sociality which would inevitably arise from correctly designed spaces and forms. Science, particularly social science, would define humanity's needs, and technical planners would meet them.

TECHNO-COSMOPOLITANISM

Let me illustrate these processes. In 1899 Tony Garnier won the coveted Prix de Rome at the Ecole des Beaux Arts competition with a neo-classical drawing of a large bank. In 1902 Garnier sent back to the guardians of the tradition at the Institut de France an unprecedented plan, *Une Cité Industrielle*. This plan has been taken as one of the central forerunners of modern planning. It embodies—although no manifesto accompanied it—the elements of the emergent modern welfare society in one paradigmatic representational "work of art."

Garnier's plan is intended as a socialist *cité* in the sense of a polis, not merely a town plan. Garnier incorporates the whole region, in keeping with the school of French historical regional geographers. The plan is not utopian, based on technically precise considerations; it was designed to be built, and in fact it was partially implemented in Lyons, where Garnier spent his working life. Garnier's plan is admittedly ambiguous. Various strains of modern planning and modern society can be found in it. Le Corbusier saw it as a precursor of high modernism. It also was taken up by socialist reformers and by "enlightened" colonialists, such as Hubert Lyautey in Morocco. This ambiguity reveals its representational and normative power.

Garnier's plan emphasized zoning; interestingly, the city's zones embody the modern ambition of spatially and representationally distributing the functions of social life. The planned city featured the following components. Work: among the planned industries were futuristic cement plants before the futurists.

Leisure and sports: the planned city would have establishments for the improvement of the body and for recuperation after work. Domestic life: the residents would live in a housing zone artfully equipped with scientifically mandated schools, child care, and medical facilities as well as pedestrian areas. Health: a sanitarium would be built on the choicest land, nestled against the hills and exposed to the most sun, and a generous number of the most advanced hospitals would care for general health and for the statistically inevitable accidents which industry would produce. Administration of the center of the city (Garnier's city had no churches and no police stations) was given over to assembly, and concert halls for public discussion of socialist culture. And history: located in the central administrative complex was an empty building, the archives. As Halbwachs, who belonged to the same reformist wing of French socialism as Garnier, was to theorize later, without collective memory there would be only the alienation of capitalism. Finally, an old town is sketchily added upriver from the industrial city, a reminder and symbol of the sedimentation of history in a socialized nature.

Morocco

One possible development of the principles of Garnier's plan was most fully carried out in Morocco, the last French colonial venture. It was in Morocco that techno-cosmopolitanism was most fully enacted. Governor-General Hubert Lyautey and his team sought to operationalize every aspect of human life from artisan crafts to hydraulics. Lyautey's technicians undertook extensive study of all dimensions of Moroccan life. This period of inquiry into North African society has been characterized as the least "Orientalist" period because of the high quality of the ethnographic and historical work produced. Lyautey's team sought to orchestrate—following the newly articulated principles and schemata of planning—these historical, cultural, and social practices and institutions into an artificial, organic whole. Lyautey was not seeking to create these elements *ex nihilio;* he believed strongly that only the historically sedimented social practices had the potential to be modernized and remain healthy. He was not a high modernist or a utopian. It is in this sense that his project can be called cosmopolitan. Although the technical principles were universal, they had to be applied in each specific case with a detailed attention to local circumstances—topography, history, power. Only then would they yield an orderly, efficient, productive, and healthy society.

Just as Garnier produced palpable representations of his *cité*, so, too, Lyautey was convinced (although he was much more explicit and sophisticated about it) that representation was a crucial factor in making the order-inducing norms a reality. The investment in representation (and consequent belief that it was possible) can be seen in the plans of Lyautey and his architect Prost (a friend and colleague of Garnier's at the Villa Medici in Rome) for the central plaza of Casablanca, where Morocco's administrative headquarters would be located. The buildings were to be constructed with the most modern of technical means in terms of construction techniques and were to serve modern aims of government. Their architectural style was an authentic pastiche style, if you will, in which elements of former Moroccan styles and decorative motifs, catalogued and systematized by Lyautey's scholars, were joined together into a neo-Moorish form. The style and the technique served the new protectorate's goal of dominating Morocco while modernizing it. During World War I, when French troops were substantially withdrawn from Morocco, Lyautey and Prost rushed ahead with the facades of these public buildings as a means of defining this new space and staking out a future politics.

THE AGGLOMERATION: TOWARD THE SOCIOTECHNICAL ENVIRONMENT

Lyautey had invested heavily in the power of forms to reinvigorate sedimented social relations and shape new ones. The leading urban reformer of the interwar period, Henri Sellier, solidly anchored in French socialist conceptions of justice and faced with many more practical constraints, came to pose the problem of the ordering of space and population in a different fashion. The object on which Sellier operated was the agglomeration. The agglomeration was no longer a territorial unit in the sense of a space defined by long-term historico-natural processes. It was no longer primarily a historico-natural milieu. Nor was it a public social-political space. Rather, it was becoming, at least discursively, a more abstract space—a socio-technical environment—in which operational transformations were regulated by specialists. The norms guiding Sellier's emerging socialist modernism were the welfare of the population, the maximization of individual potential, and their linkage through efficient administration, directed by committed specialists dedicated to the public good.

After World War I Sellier cast the problem in terms of how to mobilize political support for a flexible new administrative structure, one based on statistical projections and abstract social unities, while retaining more traditional political accountability and social linkages. For Sellier and his allies, the Parisian agglomeration formed a single socioeconomic unit. The older administrative grid, composed of the city and its surrounding communes, was not simply outmoded but positively detrimental to healthy development. For housing, for transportation, for social life in general, there was a total lack of coherent policy. The absence of any effective land policy meant that the suburbs of Paris offered inexpensive locations for industry to exploit in a socially and hygienically irresponsible manner. Such development was occurring at the expense of what Sellier called "social cost." The task was to develop techniques to combat the social plagues accompanying unregulated capitalist expansion.

Halbwachs identified the increasingly feeble fabric of social relations among workers as the chief danger facing French society. He reasoned that since modern work conditions were producing increasingly desocialized individuals, the answer to social health lay in creating the richest possible social milieu away from work. Following this logic, Sellier called on architects and urbanists as well as social scientists to produce and regulate an optimum social environment as the means to rehumanize modern life. He proposed a ring of garden cities around Paris, composed through architectural compositional methods still drawn largely from the Beaux Arts—derived urbanism, employing regional styles, and oriented toward a new type of citizen, the employee.[2]

By the mid-1930s Sellier was frustrated by lack of success, and his conceptions evolved, or better, involuted. He reluctantly placed less emphasis on local political participation and more on social scientific administration and the exigencies of cost analysis. In important ways Sellier was a transitional figure. While clinging to an older socialist symbolism (politically, historically, socially), during the course of the interwar period he gradually adopted a more modernist sociological and administrative language of self-referential form unmoored from these older referents. One can see Sellier as embodying the tensions inherent in keeping some relationship between a socialist conception of *la cité*, that public space of politics, and the agglomeration, that anonymous space of regulation and rationalization.

Planning

In the interwar period proposals abounded on the need for experts to exercise more power to overcome crippling political blockages and bring France into what was increasingly referred to as the modern world. During the 1930s there was a good deal of discussion about planning in France as in other industrial countries, and after 1935 a certain number of pro-planning politicians even held governmental positions. However, as the technical tools, statistical data, and the like required for modern planning were largely unavailable, most of the self-proclaimed plans which flourished during the interwar period were little more than manifestos. Still, they are important for creating a discursive space which would be filled during and after Vichy in a much more substantial manner.[3]

American and German models of industrial modernization fascinated a sector of the French business community and intelligentsia as early as the Universal Exposition of 1900 but attained a sustained vigor only during and after World War I. The social and political implications of Taylorism were particularly captivating to groups such as the Musée Social, an early advocate of its introduction into diverse realms of French life. On the Left, Edouard Herriot proposed a technologically inspired Fourth Republic as a means of overcoming the continuing parliamentary blockages of what he perceived to be France's national interest. Henri Fayol and the movement for management reform advocated molding the state in the image of a new, efficient industrial apparatus. Fayol's dramatic proposals—to transfer state bureaucracies to private hands—were not followed, but new management methods were instituted to some extent in both French business and government. The main institutional enthusiasts for planning ideas during the interwar period were the unions, particularly the leftist CGT, convinced that experiments during the war had demonstrated the compatibility of industrial productivity, higher wages, and improved negotiating power for workers.[4]

Before World War I the French public sector, largely inherited from the *ancien régime* except for the railroads, consisted mainly of artistic workshops. The government, consistent with liberal doctrine, had no program for economic management and lacked the data and analytic tools to invent one. This situation changed dramatically during World War I. The role of the state expanded at unprecedented rates: military expenditures exploded such that service on the debt exceeded the entire prewar budget. Disparate conceptions of how to orchestrate and make the relations of state and industry more efficient and productive competed within the government during the war. Organizational methods, the information necessary to carry them out, and political strategies to implement them took a leap forward in complexity. However, in France many of these "modernized" institutional arrangements were dismantled immediately after the war. The key players—cartelized industrialists, politicians, a small group of bureaucrats who had become specialists in navigating between the conflicting institutional forces of French society, and believers in the new techniques of understanding and regulation—remained on the scene in an uneasy relationship during the interwar years.[5]

Description

Urban description in the interwar years vacillated between an organic and a mechanical set of metaphors. The term "function," taken over from the biologists and geographers, shakily bridged the metaphoric field. On the mechanist side Leon Jaussely argued that the economic organization of the city should be considered as the "Taylorization of a vast workshop, where for the most precise reasons, each thing had a precise reason for being in one and only one place."[6] He provided a kind of manifesto in the first issue of *La Vie urbaine*. Urbanism grew out of geography. Geographers provided two essential tools: first, the detailed and comprehensive analysis of *genre de vie*; second, the technical means of representing these givens in a standard form. Jaussely claimed that the life of a city in its entirety could be reproduced through graphic means, and almost entirely on a series of exact plans drawn to the same scale. Jaussely produced maps of climatic conditions, topography, demography, historical influence, social and professional locations, ethnic groups, population movement, economic activity, circulation patterns, public and private spaces, construction, overcrowded housing, death and morbidity rates, and traffic accidents. Combining this swirl of variables into a single plan required a complexity of presentation that Jaussely barely intuited.[7]

On the organicist side Louis Bonnier compared the city with a living organism evolving in space and time. Bonnier proposed to study Paris as a spatial distribution of a population, one which ignored older arbitrary administrative distinctions drawn up for historical reasons relating to political or military considerations, not ones of population per se.[8] Bonnier presented a series of remarkable maps showing the spatial growth of the Parisian agglomeration as well as the changing densities of specific areas. Population, Bonnier argued, occupied a different space than politics; Jaussely would have added that economics did as well. Uniting all the variables into a common field required new conceptions of space and society and a new understanding of how to bring them into a common frame.

Garden Cities and Human Material

Sellier and his allies fought for a planned, socially hygienic, and aesthetically coordinated series of garden cities coordinated with public housing development in Paris itself. Sellier's strategy for the Parisian agglomeration turned on land acquisition by the communes and coordination efforts in all domains by his office at the departmental level. This strategy implied two important innovations: state intervention in the definition of change, and identification of the need to invent and then plan for the placement of new social unities. The lead article of the 1923 issue of *La Vie urbaine* was a report by Sellier on the International Conference on Garden Cities and Urban Planning, held in Paris in October 1922.[9] Sellier urged the creation of a series of satellite garden-city settlements. He admired the English accomplishments but was opposed to literal imitations, especially of the ideal of self-contained satellite cities. Ebenezer Howard's vision could not serve directly as a model for France because it planned for cities separate from large agglomerations. One might say that for Sellier, the English put too much emphasis on the garden and not enough on the city. For Sellier, the suburb was urban.

Despite the sociological inconvenience, Sellier favored retaining the commune as a baseline unit because of its historical significance as well as the social and political anchorage it provided for *la cité*. For political reasons Sellier opposed the creation of a single unified commune, which he feared would drown out the voices of elected officials and give a totally free hand to administration. Democracy required a local, socially grounded counter-voice to governmental bureaucracy. When such a counterweight was weak, it needed to be strengthened; when it was absent entirely, it needed to be invented.

Although the importance of industry was primary, Sellier paid very little explicit attention to it.[10] What images there were of work were largely negative: work and its sites were tiring, polluted, noisy, ugly, unhealthy. Just as there was no valorization of working-class sociality per se or revolutionary politics, so, too, there was no reform project for industry. Sellier's counter-image was peace and calm after work. This humanism was meant literally: a refusal of working-class isolation and brutalization as well as an affirmation of a modern, socialist republican citizenry. To explain this compensatory, rehabilatory stance toward modern work, we turn to Maurice Halbwachs.

Halbwachs, in his "Matière et société," presented one of the first French theories of alienation, and in good Durkheimian fashion gave primacy to social factors rather than economic ones. Halbwachs defined industrial workers as that group of men who, "in order to carry out their jobs, must orient themselves toward matter and leave society behind."[11] He proceeded through an ingenious demonstration showing how industrial workers' representations of themselves and others were mediated by matter and how this mediation deformed the workers' representations of both nature and society. The natural tendency to value the picturesque in nature grasped as a whole and the inherent value of social relations in a social whole was reduced to "sensations mechanically associated in a closed series."[12] The opposite of this situation, the norm of social health, as it were, was social life at its most intense—urban life—where both nature and culture were appreciated fully for their social worth.

The supposed advances in industrial relations were accelerating this negative process, not improving it. The introduction of Taylorism refined the decomposition of social relations. On the one hand, it enforced the standardization of all individuality among workers; on the other hand, the introduction of management specialists who did not share skills or social life with the workers marked an important loss of autonomy for the industrial worker. The result was to increase desocialization. The industrial worker in modern society increasingly formed representations of himself along an axis of inanimate matter, one which led him away from society. The situation of salaried employees was only marginally better. Halbwachs showed how their status was determined by their general lack of independence, initiative, and responsibility. As was the case with the rest of the emerging middle classes, their work was characterized by an ambiguous technicity. These people applied predefined rules to specified situations, but little more was demanded or permitted of them. This "materialized humanity" only followed the great tides of social change in a dominated fashion. Their situation was an ambiguous one, neither fully dominated nor dominant. Halbwachs approvingly quotes Tocqueville on the spirit of the middle classes as one which mixes that of the people and the aristocracy; such a spirit can produce miracles, but by itself it would never produce a government or civilization of virtue and grandeur. Clearly Halbwachs felt that a vision of social justice and techniques to implement it were needed to save the new employees from mediocrity or worse.

Socialist Social Space

Sellier's concern for creating new forms of social bonds—in many ways parallel to Lyautey's conceptions of pacification except that the groups to be pacified were not yet in existence—was explicitly developed in a 1922 article in *La Vie urbaine*, "Les centres sociaux dans les regions rurales aux Etats-Unis." Sellier pointed to American small town or rural innovations which he believed could be applied in France to urban agglomerations.[13] Sellier was enthusiastic about the American experience of rural civic centers. They were excellent devices for the development of social life, promising to preserve and revitalize both rural habitation and population. Sellier valorized the sheer intensification of social activity per se. Once a combination of economic activity and civic administration was set in place, and once a space was created, new and healthy social unities would emerge, and older ones would be stabilized and regenerated. Although the functioning and financing of these civic centers varied a great deal, they all shared a number of common features. At a minimum they all contained an auditorium (with folding chairs) available for multiple purposes from banquets to speeches and a kitchen; in larger towns they might boast a cafe, billiards room, library, and visiting room for the county health officer and agricultural agent as well as the chamber of commerce.

Sellier knew that parallel spaces existed in French cities. The Maison Commune or Maison pour Tous was a transformation of the earlier socialist Bourse du Travail or Social Catholic Foyer social spaces. It became a characteristic form of the new French interwar cities, especially (if not uniquely) in the socialist municipalities. It has been called the major socialist "equipmental" contribution. A simply constructed but large building, in small towns placed next to sports facilities, should house a library, a sewing room for women, child care facilities and *une buvette de temperance*.[14] Often placed at the city's symbolic center, it embodied hopes for new modern civilization, the best of politics, education, and culture. The idea of an autonomous social space, neither directly a governmental building nor a private mercantile amusement space, had a complex history throughout the nineteenth century. Jean-Louis Cohen (in the spirit of Halbwachs) argues that it would be naive to reduce the production of these spaces entirely to reformers' projects; they corresponded to social demands as well. The changing position of fortresses of union activity to a broader and more diffuse place of sociability (and of education) occurred slowly but surely as the Left assimilated the existence of the Third Republic and vice versa.[15]

Sellier's aim was to provide the cadre for a renewed modern sociality. Sellier's consistent goal (one he never achieved) was to make garden cities complete social cells, composed of inhabitants from a wide range of social categories, thus avoiding an unhealthy isolation stemming from the irrational development of cities and their consequent class hostility. He fully accepted the principle of different classes of housing for different social categories. Part of the division of classes in the garden cities was linked to the ground rent idea: fancier houses, higher taxes, more housing and services. Sellier was not alone in this acceptance of the spatial separation of classes. The only two French projects in the first half of the century which do not program explicit social class differences were Tony Garnier's *Une Cité industrielle* and Le Corbusier's *Une Cité radieuse*. Neither really addressed the problem: Garnier was planning to accommodate only one class, while Le Corbusier's standards were universalistic, the *l'homme-type*.

Sellier, following Halbwachs, was guided by a norm of social life in which the mixing of classes intensified the representations of society. He thought the working class, the salaried employees, and the lower middle classes were precisely those social groups most in need of a rich, independent social setting, one in which the picturesque had an important function to play. He envisioned garden cities as a quarter or neighborhood, a part capable of sensing specific needs in the best possible manner but not cut off from the city. This principle was important: neither Sellier nor the Conseil General de la Seine sought to destroy Paris; they meant instead to preserve it by relieving the conditions of congestion, by creating urban suburbs as part of a new agglomeration. The garden city was to be neither a complete city nor a suburban scattering of individual houses, but a social unity, attached to an urban center, improved according to the latest principles, assembling diverse social categories, devoted to strengthening, social exchanges, solidarity, and moral bonds.

Suresnes

As Sellier was mayor of Suresnes, it was an obvious candidate for the implementation of his plans. For well over a thousand years the village of Suresnes, on the western outskirts of Paris, had lived from its vineyards. During the seventeenth century it became a fashionable site of aristocratic houses; the Rothschilds built a mansion there in the nineteenth. By the end of the nineteenth century, as with other suburbs around Paris, a railroad linked Suresnes to Paris; the village was transforming itself into an industrial site. The Rothschilds built a steel tube factory; a bicycle factory set up shop; then the first automaker (Darracq in 1905). Others followed: aviation motors; an electricity plant (Westinghouse), an important perfume factory. By the end of the nineteenth century Suresnes's population had grown to eleven thousand. Although some vineyards were still active, its future lay elsewhere.[16]

Following Sellier's ideas, the plan for Suresnes sought to orient a preexisting evolutionary development. The garden city of Suresnes was to be built on thirty hectares acquired by the Department of the Seine adjacent to the existing town. The study of the site was followed by a general design of the whole. Within this whole, elements (streets, squares, edifices, houses, trees, sports fields, schools, shops, communal buildings) were distributed according to the urbanist's art. Services were literally embodied in functionally specific buildings deployed as morphological elements. Symbolically, social services were given a central localization. They formed the focus of the city's circulation system and in large part took the place of monuments. Sellier's team paid particular attention to educational and hygienic services as well as new spaces for modern social life. For Suresnes three main zones were delimited: an industrial zone in which housing was discouraged; a residential zone reserved for individual houses and small businesses; and a model garden city guided by strict modern health considerations of maximum light and building controls. The plan called for 1,300 lodgings distributed in 550 individual houses grouped around gardens and 750 lodgings in collective houses of three to four stories grouped along the main thoroughfares. The plan allowed for three to five rooms for each family, with running water, electricity, gas, a garage, and even central heating for some. In Suresnes, Sellier introduced cooperatives of consumption and production, mutualist restaurants and pharmacies. Community centers were included in the plans for almost all the garden cities.

It was no accident that most of the proposed garden city sites were located adjacent to older towns. Whenever Sellier spoke of the "cities of tomorrow," he almost always evoked an older preserved core and a periphery organized along modern planning principles but maintaining strong ties with the older city. In the first issue of the *Bulletin de la Société Historique de Suresnes* (1920) Sellier argued for the importance of preserving some of the old quarters of Suresnes to conserve a sense of its identity. The old city played a historical, touristic role and kept alive the city's character, the specificity of its culture. Sellier and his friend Marcel Poëte had together established a course on urbanism and the history of Paris at the Ecole Pratique des Hautes Etudes, which stressed the importance of local historical determinants in the definition, growth, and future of cities. Sellier took its scientific importance quite literally. Before establishing the plan for Suresnes, Sellier undertook a detailed study of the commune's evolution. He wrote an article for the first issue of the historical society's annual bulletin entitled "The Future of Suresnes Tied to Its Past," which chronicled the town's growth, its periods of health and decline. An enlightened municipal administration understood that in urban evolution as in biology there was always a high price to be paid for a brutal rupture between the past and the present. In this belief Sellier remained firmly rooted in techno-cosmopolitanism.

Historical discourse also had additional roles to play. The Historical Society of Suresnes was used by Sellier as a means for building consensus or at least communicating with potentially hostile social groups and local notables in Suresnes. It also served to establish him as a historical figure in his own right. During a period of intense change, the discourse of history became a privileged medium of communication. In 1926 Sellier met and enthusiastically supported local initiatives for an artistic and historical society. He welcomed the idea of a *fête municipale*, and the municipality financially supported these efforts to build a consensus on Suresnes's past and present. Although former comrades in the Communist party criticized his participation with church leaders and industrialists, Sellier was conscious of the need to broaden his political and social base. Historical discourse, as a promoter of both unity and division, has played an extremely central role in French life.[17] Sellier had learned, and learned to practice, a "heroic" history of the exemplary figures of the Left. He transformed this mode of historical moralizing into a legitimizing discourse for his own social policies; he often cited Saint Vincent de Paul's charitable works in Suresnes, and frequently cited his "name-sake" Henri IV. Sellier appeared in the pages of the association's bulletin as the patron of Suresnes, without mention of political party. The society contributed to making him a legend, hoping to form a consensus around his person if not his ideas.

The Social-Technical Environment: Middling Modernism

In 1938 Louis Boulonnois, one of Sellier's chief counselors in Suresnes, published *L'Oeuvre municipale de M. Henri Sellier à Suresnes*, which can be considered an official presentation of Sellier's program in its final form.[18] Boulonnois, who referred to Sellier as "Maître," had been a school teacher in Suresnes before joining Sellier's administration. Married to one of Suresnes's new corps of social workers, he might be characterized as a fully integrated member and apostle of the new reformist socialist administration. Although by 1938 Sellier himself was increasingly bitter, Boulonnois remained optimistic. The goal was no longer limited to meeting housing needs or even to the systematic distribution of welfare institutions throughout the city, although, as Sellier was keenly aware, these objectives were far from having been attained. By the mid-1930s a complementary task (sketchily present in Sellier's earlier projects) had been brought to center stage: to reach out from public buildings to institute a comprehensive program of physical and moral preventive care to cure social ills. The priority was no longer the isolation and rectification of islands of pathology; rather, the new program amounted to a blueprint for the scientific administration of modern life as a whole.

The new objectives of municipal organization were to predict and prepare for accidents and to specify needs—put most broadly, to prepare the instruments of social defense. Although programs served the public good, Boulonnois saw his role as technical rather than political. Care of the collectivity fell to administration, these technicians argued with a beguiling understatement, because the ordinary citizen, preoccupied with the details of day-to-day life, all too frequently neglected to plan ahead. Administration's role as arbiter and planner might not always be appreciated by the average citizen, but that ingratitude was the price to be paid for the larger public good, whose self-appointed guardian Boulonnois and associates had become. *Prevoyance* had moved from being the individual moral virtue par excellence to be inculcated by discipline and surveillance, to being a normalizing administrative function guided by science and operating on a population. The transition to technocratic modernism would be completed when the population's norms of health became functions of the instruments of measurement themselves.

Boulonnois argued that the role of administration was the scientific arbitration of social conflict. Successful management entailed more comprehensive and sophisticated knowledge of the population (particularly its range of differences and its future development) as well as more flexible, more continuous, more far-sighted means of administering its needs. The ideal target population for scientific administration, he argued, was one still in a molten social state, that is, not fixed in its historical, geographical, or social milieu. It was public service which, in the last instance, was charged with analyzing, producing, and directing a new social solidarity among these new men. The symbol "plan" provided Boulonnois with the metaphoric bridge to connect social organization with the individual. His penchant for slogans served him well in this instance; he presented the task as "To bestow on the allotments a city plan [*un plan de ville*], and symmetrically on the assisted families a life plan [*un plan de vie*]."[19] This was no longer a project of regulating and ameliorating a locale and its inhabitants but of treating both as matter to be formed and normed literally at will or, more accurately, through a thoroughly voluntarist program—pure middling modernist totalization and individualization.

In this discourse, society, the government, and the individual were potentially transparent to one another. To achieve the articulation between these institutions and the population, social facts had to be brought into a standardized grid. This process entailed an objective and objectifying vocabulary for individual and social needs as well as a functionalist understanding of institutions. To this technician's vision of social reality was attached a conception of the state as a set of bureaus whose job was to deliver functionally specific public services—roads, water, agriculture, hygiene, housing—and to provide a "steering mechanism" for the whole society. Although Boulonnois's proposals were formed as part of a socialist humanist project, Vichy and subsequent French regimes carried out a parallel project for the state, albeit with different aims.

The central locus for the intersection of the macro- and micro-knowledges and powers was probably housing, although it is important to emphasize that social housing was in the process of being redefined as an abstract question of technical spaces and scientifically established needs rather than as a specifically disciplinary concern. In 1934, for example, an international effort was set in motion to establish a homogeneous typology of housing. These standards were adopted for the census to permit a standardized analysis of needs, a more substantial base for prevision. Concurrent with the establishment of these technical standards (and organizing them) was a set of normalizing criteria for their usage. Norms and means were now joined. These norms of sociability were based on *la famille normale moyenne,* a stable and rational household. The norms not only classified families but also served as the basis of intervention to hasten their creation and stabilization. However, the criteria for identifying normality were not static; the scientific definition of needs was constantly being reevaluated. Further, families who failed to qualify for housing were not definitively eliminated from the pool but, rather, were offered the possibility of consulting with social workers and reapplying. Once they aligned their practices with those of the scientifically defined and selected normal community, they might qualify for housing.

Boulonnois urged his colleagues to replace the older humiliating investigations with a more precise understanding of community needs as well as a feeling of solidarity with those who failed to meet the standards. The links between the administration, its technical experts, and the population whose welfare it protected operated as a new social division of work, the norm and means of a new social solidarity. The scientifically cautioned conditions of habitation established the means for the extension of the normalization process. The administration defined the normal use of a house, making it the condition for occupation. For example, the functions of rooms were specified; the size of apartments was determined by family size (with specified upper limits); and modern conveniences like gas and electricity were required. As a consequence, the plan called for regular payment not only of rent but also of gas bills; gave social workers the right to enter houses to check hygiene; and established an obligatory system of insurance. All these improvements and regulations implied a regular salary and reinforced the regulation of regular habits. Many of these criteria were not new, but given the new administrative structure, they led gradually to state measures (in relation to a normal family) used to establish rent, state subventions, and so on. Various systems of control were put in place in accord with these normalized and scientific standards: obligatory visits to the public baths, weekly visits from social workers who established typical household budgets, and the like.

Universalizing norms and a system of stratification gradually displaced the class-based disciplinary tactics of hygiene as well as environmentalist localisms in defining and enforcing a new social reality. The bacteriological and class phase was passing to a functionalist and normalizing sociological one. Once the normalized *mode de vie* became a category defined in terms of *niveau de vie*, the surpluses added to it became the basis of a differential status. The older class and "type" understanding was giving way to a stratification and "distinction" grid.[20] During the course of the 1920s and 1930s the object of intervention slowly shifted from city planning to the management of *la matière sociale*. Instead of a functionally harmonized urbanity, Sellier and his team were constrained by their political weakness and worsening economic conditions to limit, grudgingly and gradually, the scope of their interventions to perfecting specific social spaces and social sciences.

The loss involved, the diminished social and socialist vision, was dearer to Sellier than to his followers. Sellier's assistants became almost evangelistic spokespersons for the creation of modernized tools of sociological analysis of needs and norms of life as well as enthusiastic participants in the invention of social actors to implement these new techniques. While Sellier clung to history and locale as sources of legitimacy and solidarity, his younger assistants and successors were perhaps more consistent, gradually stripping away such architectural, historical, and social references in the name of efficiency, science, progress, and welfare. Georges Canguilhem, analyzing a parallel change in psychology, characterizes it as a shift from utilitarianism—utility for man—to instrumentalism, man as an instrument of utility. This sea change in techniques, objects, and goals constituted a shift from a search for means of adaptation to a historico-natural milieu to the creation of an appropriate socio-technical one.[21]

NOTES

1. Paul Rabinow, *French Modern: Norms and Forms of the Social Environment* (Chicago: University of Chicago Press, 1995; orig. 1989).

2. Georges Teyssot, "Civilisation du salarie et culture de l'employé: Variations sur Siegfried Kracauer, Ernst Bloch et Walter Benjamin," *Les Cahiers de la recherche architecturale* 15–17 (1985): 36–41.

3. For a detailed discussion of neosocialist alternatives, see Zeev Sternhell, *Ni droite ni gauche: L'Ideologie fasciste en France* (Paris, 1983).

4. Charles S. Maier, "Between Taylorism and Technocracy: European Ideologies and the Vision of Industrial Productivity in the 1920s," *Journal of Contemporary History* 5, no. 2 (1970); Henri Le Chatelier, *Le Taylorisme*, 2d ed. (Paris: Dunnod, 1934). Thanks to Mary McLeod for her thesis and her helpful comments and discussions.

5. Richard F. Kuisel, *Capitalism and the State in Modern France: Renovation and Economic Management in the Twentieth Century* (Cambridge, U.K.: Cambridge University Press, 1981); Martin Fine, "Toward Corporatism: The Movement for Capital-Labor Collaboration in France, 1914–1936," Ph.D. diss., University of Wisconsin, Madison, 1971. John F. Godfrey, *Capitalism at War: Industrial Policy and Bureaucracy in France, 1914–1918* (Leamington Spa, U.K.: Berg, 1987).

6. Leon Jaussely, preface to *L'Etude pratique des plans de villes* , by Raymond Unwin (Paris: Librairie Centrale des Beaux-arts, 1922), p. vii.

7. Leon Jaussely, "Chronique de l'urbanisme," *La Vie urbaine*, nos. 1–2 (March–June 1919): 184–85.

8. Louis Bonnier, "La population de Paris en mouvement, 1800–1861," *La Vie urbaine*, nos. 1–2 (March–June 1919): 8.

9. Henri Sellier, "Conference internationale des cités-jardins et de l'aménagement des villes," *La Vie urbaine*, no. 18 (15 February 1923): 11–21.

10. On the history of this theme, see Jean-Pierre Epron, ed., "L'Usine et la ville 1836–1986: 150 ans d'urbanisme," *Culture Technique* (Spring 1986).

11. Maurice Halbwachs, "Matière et société," in *Classes sociales et morphologie*, ed. V. Karady (Paris: Minuit, 1972), p. 60.

12. Ibid., p. 68.

13. Henri Sellier, "Les centres sociaux dans les regions rurales aux Etats-

Unis," *La Vie urbaine*, no. 4 (1922): 1.

14. Donat-Alfred Agache, J. M. Auburtin, and E. Redont, *Comment Reconstruire nos cités détruites* (Paris: Colin, 1915).

15. Jean-Louis Cohen, "Des bourses du travail au temps des loisirs les avatars de la sociabilité ouvrière," in his *Architecture pour le people* (Brussels: Archives de l'Architecture Moderne, 1984), p. 159.

16. René Sordes, *Histoire de Suresnes* (Suresnes: Societé Historique de Suresnes, 1965), pp. 460–75.

17. For an extensive literature, see Pierre Nora, ed., *Les Lieux de memoire*, vol. 1 (Paris: Gallimard, 1984).

18. Louis Boulonnois, *L'Oeuvre municipale de M. Henri Sellier à Suresnes* (Paris: Berger-Lerrault, 1938).

19. Ibid., p. 80.

20. Pierre Bourdieu, *La Distinction, critique sociale du jugement* (Paris: Editions du Minuit, 1979).

21. Georges Canguilhem, "Qu'est-ce que la psychologie," in his *Etudes d'histoire et de philosophie des sciences* (Paris: Vrin, 1983), pp. 378–79.

CHAPTER 4

Georges Canguilhem: A Vital Rationalist

GEORGES CANGUILHEM was born in Castelnaudary in southwestern France in 1904. Although his father was a tailor, Canguilhem liked to refer to himself, not without a certain twinkle in his eye, as of peasant stock, rooted in the harmonious, cyclical life of the soil and the seasons, his sensibilities formed by the yearly round of the fruit trees. The story of his sentimental education is a classic one; his high marks on national examinations sent him on a journey to the Paris to study. Once there, he certainly was a success. After completing his studies at the prestigious Lycée Henri IV, he then entered the pinnacle of elite educational institutions in France, the Ecole Normale Supérieure, in 1924. Among his *promotion*, his cohort, were Jean-Paul Sartre, Raymond Aron, and Paul Nizan. Maurice Merleau-Ponty entered a year later. Already at this time, Canguilhem was interested in themes that he would continually return to and develop throughout his intellectual life: in specific, a paper on Auguste Comte's theory of order and progress, submitted for a diploma, displays the beginnings of this tenacious, yet constantly renewed interest in the relations of reason and society. The philosopher Alain's 1924 judgment of Canguilhem as "lively, resolute and content" (*vif, resolu et content*) captured the man's spirit almost three-quarters of a century later.[1]

Once he became *agrégé* in philosophy in 1927, the young Canguilhem began his teaching tour of provincial *lycées* as was required of all Ecole Normale graduates in repayment to the state for their education. His initial peregrinations ended in Toulouse, in 1936, where he stayed until 1940 because, as he told an interviewer, he hadn't become an *agrégé* in philosophy in order to teach the doctrine of the Vichy regime.[2] He took advantage of this newly found free time to complete his medical studies. Prophetically, in both a philosophic and political sense, Canguilhem replaced the philosopher of mathematics, Jean Cavaillès (who was called to the Sorbonne) at the University of Strasbourg, whose faculty relocated to Clermont-Ferrand in 1941 when Strasbourg was annexed by the Hitlerian Reich. He was present at the formation of an important resistance group to which Canguilhem's medical skills were made available. A life in the century, as the French say, meaning that Canguilhem, like so many of his compatriots, had his life shaped by the conjuncture of France's enduring institutions and the contingent events of his time.

In 1943 Canguilhem defended his medical thesis. The continued timeliness of this work is attested to by the daunting durability of that 1943 thesis, *The Normal and the Pathological*.[3] After the war, he took up his post at the University of Strasbourg (in Strasbourg) where he remained until 1948. After first refusing the important administrative post of *inspecteur général de philosophie* in philosophy at the liberation, he finally accepted it in 1948, serving until 1955 when he accepted the Chair of History and Philosophy of Sciences at the Sorbonne. Canguilhem also succeeded Gaston Bachelard as director of the Institut d'Histoire des sciences et des techniques. His reputation as a ferocious examiner lives on in Paris today, as does a deep well of affection for the intellectual and institutional support he provided over the decades.[4]

History and Philosophy of Science

Louis Althusser paid Canguilhem a compliment when he compared him (as well as Cavaillès, Bachelard, Vuillemin, and Foucault) to an anthropologist who goes into the field armed with "a scrupulous respect for the reality of real science."[5] The statement is revealing, if not quite an accurate description of Canguilhem's method. The more strictly ethnographic studies of laboratory life associated with the name of Bruno Latour would come later and would aim not merely at correcting a positivist and idealist understanding of science as a single unified activity achieving a cumulative understanding of nature, but at dismantling the very idea of science—a position as far from Canguilhem's as one could imagine. Nonetheless, Althusser's statement captures the move, first initiated by Bachelard, away from the static universalism which the French university system had enshrined in its rationalist and idealist approaches to science. For Bachelard, philosophy's new role was to analyze the historical development of the truth-producing practices. Philosophy of science became the study of regional epistemologies, of historical reflection on the elaboration of theories and concepts by practicing scientists, physicists, chemists, pathologists, anatomists, etc.

Canguilhem is clear and adamant that even though philosophy was no longer sovereign and autonomous, it still had important work to accomplish. Unlike the scientist, the epistemologist's problem is to establish "the order of conceptual progress that is visible only after the fact and of which the present notion of scientific truth is the provisional point of culmination."[6] Truths are found in the practices of science. Philosophy analyzes their plurality and historicity, consequently their provisionality, while affirming—not legislating as the older French philosophy of science attempted to do—their normativity. Epistemology is a rigorous description of the process by which truth is elaborated, not a list of final results. Althusser's encomium takes for granted that science exists and has a privileged status; Canguilhem, like Foucault and Bourdieu, never doubted this: "To take as one's object of inquiry nothing other than sources, inventions, influences, priorities, simultaneities, and successions is at bottom to fail to distinguish between science and other aspects of culture."[7] This assumption—Bruno Latour has called it the key symbol of French philosophy and history of science—is the linchpin of the architecture of the house of reason inhabited by Canguilhem.[8] Science, for Canguilhem, is "a discourse verified in a delimited sector of experience."[9] Science is an exploration of the norm of rationality at work. But just as firm as the belief in science is the belief in its multiple historicities. There are only diverse sciences at work at particular historical moments: physics is not biology; eighteenth-century natural history is not twentieth-century genetics.

For Canguilhem, "The history of sciences is the history of an object which is a history, which has a history, while science is the science of an object which isn't history and which doesn't have a history."[10] Science, through its use of method, divides nature into objects. These objects are in a sense secondary but not derivative ones; one could say they are both constructed and discovered. The history of science performs a similar set of operations on scientific objects. The object of historical discourse is "the historicity of scientific discourse, in so much as that history effectuates a project guided by its own internal norms but traversed by accidents . . . interrupted by crises, that is to say by moments of judgment and truth."[11] These truths are always contestable, and in process, but no less "real" on account of their contingency The history of science is not natural history. It does not identify the science with the scientist, the scientists with their biographies, or sciences with their results, and the results with their current pedagogic use. The epistemological and historical claims here are magisterial and run counter to much of contemporary *doxa* in the social studies of science.[12]

The Normal and the Pathological

Although Canguilhem had published a traditional philosophical treatise on ethics, *Traité de logique et de morale,* intended as a textbook for advanced *lycée* students, in the late 1930s, the work for which he is known starts with his thesis. The work's central theme is announced in the title, *The Normal and the Pathological.* His work signaled a major reversal in thinking about health. Previously, French medical training had privileged the normal; disease or malfunction was understood as the deviation from a fixed norm. Such norms were taken to be constants. Medical practice was directed at scientifically establishing these norms and, practice following theory, toward returning the patient to health, to reestablishing the norm from which the patient had strayed.

As the philosopher of biology François Dagognet crisply observed, Canguilhem "launched a frontal attack on 'that edifice of normalization' so essential to the procedures of a positivist science and medicine."[13] He did so by re-posing the question of the organism as a living being in an environment with which there was no preestablished harmony. Suffering, not normative measurements and standard deviations, established the state of disease. Normativity began with the living being , and with that being came diversity. Each patient a doctor treats presents a different case. Each case displays its own particularity. One of Canguilhem's famous aphorisms drives this point home: "An anomaly is not an abnormality. Diversity does not signify sickness." With living beings, normality is an activity, not a steady state. The result, if one follows Canguilhem's reasoning, is that "a number, even a constant number, translates a style, habits, a civilization, even the underlying vitality of life."[14] The recent discovery that our body temperature has a much wider range of normality than previously assumed demonstrates this point. Normality, and this is one of Canguilhem's constant themes, means the ability to adapt to changing circumstances, to variable and varying environments. Illness is a reduction to constants, the very norms by which we measure ourselves as normal. Normality equals activity and flexibility. Hence there is no purely objective pathology; rather, the basic unit is a living being in shifting relations with a changing environment. Arguing for a dramatic reversal, Canguilhem maintained that illness is ultimately defined by the terms that had defined health, namely stable norms, unchanging values.[15] Life is not stasis, not a fixed set of natural laws set in advance and the same for all, to which one must adhere in order to survive. Life is action, mobility and pathos, the constant but only partially successful effort to resist death, to use Bichat's famous definition of life as the ensemble of functions deployed to resist death.

Canguilhem's work has been a consistent and disciplined historical demonstration, a laying out of the consequences, of these principles. Life has its specificity. "Life, whatever form it may take, involves self-preservation by means of self-regulation."[16] This specificity can, in fact, must be perpetually elaborated but it can never be evaded. Canguilhem's punctuate, historical essays are not a philosophy of life like those of Hans Jonas or Maurice Merleau-Ponty which seeks to fix an understanding of life with one set of concepts. Rather, Canguilhem's tightly written didactic forays display how the life sciences, including the therapeutic ones, have simultaneously elaborated concepts of life and how these concepts must be seen as an integrated part of the phenomenon under study, life and its norms.

Although he has been vigilant not to turn these explorations into a panegyric of vitalism, Canguilhem demonstrates the constant presence of evaluative notions like 'preservation', 'regulation,' 'adaptation,' 'normality,' in both the everyday and scientific approaches to life. "It is life itself, and not medical judgment which makes the biological normal a concept of value and not a concept of statistical reality."[17] Man's specificity is not that he is separate from the rest of nature but only that Man has created systematic knowledge and tools to help him cope. This testing, parrying with pathology, this active relation to the environment, this normative mobility and projective ability—man's conceptual career—is central to his health. "Being healthy means being not only normal in a given situation but also normative in this and other eventual situations. What characterizes health is the possibility of transcending the norm, which defines the momentary normal, the possibility of tolerating infractions of the habitual norm and instituting new norms in new situations."[18] Life is an activity that follows a norm. But health is not being normal; health is being normative.

In general, reflecting on the relationships of concepts and life requires clarification regarding the fact that at least two distinct orders are being investigated. First, there is life as form, life as the 'universal organization of matter,' and second, there is life as the experience of a singular living being who is conscious of his or her life. By life one could mean the French present participle, of the verb "to live," *le vivant*, or the past participle *le vécu*. Canguilhem is unequivocal: the first level (form) controls the second (experience). It is only the first level, the power and form-giving dimensions of life, which constitutes the explicit subject matter of his work, but the presence of the second is frequently felt.[19] For all its declarative clarity the claim of priority only thinly masks the keen awareness of suffering and searching, in a word—pathos—which is the experiential double, the constant companion, of Canguilhem's insistent conceptualism. The pathos of existence is always close at hand for this physician *cum* philosopher *cum* pedagogue.

In fact, a not so latent existentialism, albeit of a distinctive and idiosyncratic sort, shadows Canguilhem's conception of medicine. One easily hears echoes of Sartre and Merleau-Ponty's early themes transferred to a different register and played in a distinctive tonality. Canguilhem's variants of "to freedom condemned" and "the structure of comportment" are composed in a different key. Canguilhem's individual is condemned to adapt to an environment and to act using concepts and tools which have no pre-established affinities with his surrounding world. Reason and life are intertwined, not opposed, but neither legislates the other. "Life becomes a wily, supple intelligence of the world, while reason, for its part, emerges as something more vital: it finally develops a logic that is more than a mere logic of identity."[20]

A New Understanding of Life: Error

It has become a commonplace to say that Georges Canguilhem's recognition by an English-speaking public, beyond a few specialists in the history of the life sciences, follows in the wake of the success of one of his favorite students and friends, Michel Foucault. Although not exactly false, such an appreciation is insufficient unless it asks what it was in Canguilhem's work which interested Foucault. Canguilhem's work, it is worth underlining, is pertinent for diverse reasons. The question to be asked then is: "Why read him today?" The answer lies partially in the other commonplace most frequently repeated. Canguilhem's predecessor, Gaston Bachelard, invented a method for a new history of the "hard sciences" of chemistry, physics, and math; his student, Michel Foucault, worked on the "dubious sciences" of Man; Canguilhem has spent his life tracing the liniments of a history of the concepts of the sciences of life. Let us suggest that today it is the biosciences with a renewed elaboration of such concepts of norms and life, death and information, which hold center stage in the scientific and social arena—hence the renewed relevance of Georges Canguilhem.

In his 1966 essay, "The New Understanding of Life," Canguilhem analyzed the contemporary revolution underway in genetics and molecular biology. The essay, a historical *tour de force*, traces the concept of life as form (and experience) as well as knowledge of that form, from Aristotle to the present. Canguilhem demonstrates the continuity of problematization and the discontinuity of answers in the history of the concept of life. This historical reconstruction provides the groundwork for an analysis of our contemporary conceptualization of life. Canguilhem frames Watson and Crick's discovery of the structure of the double helix as an information system, one in which the code and the (cellular) milieu are in constant interaction. There is no simple one-way determination from genes to effects. The new understanding of life lies not in the structuration of matter and the regulation of functions, but in a shift of scale and location: from mechanics to information and communication theory.[21] In an important sense, the new understanding of life as information rejoins Aristotle insofar as it understands life as a *logos* "inscribed, converted and transmitted" within living matter.[22] However, we have come a long way since Aristotle. The telos of life most commonly proposed today is more ethological, seeing behavior as determined and humans more as animals, than a contemplative one which assigns a special place to reflection and uncertainty. From sociobiologists to many advocates of the human genome project, the code is the central dogma.

Canguilhem rejects this telos. If *Homo sapiens* were as tightly programmed as the ethologists (or many molecular biologists) think, then how, Canguilhem asks, can we explain error, the history of errors and the history of our victories over error? Genetic errors are now understood as information errors. Among such errors, however, a large number arise from a maladaption to a milieu. Once again he reintroduces the theme of normality as situated action, not a pre-given condition. Mankind makes mistakes, it places itself in the wrong relationship with the environment, in the wrong place to receive the information needed to survive, to act, to flourish. We must move, err, adapt to survive. This condition, of "erring or drift," is not merely accidental or external to life but its fundamental form. Knowledge, following this understanding of life, is "a disquieting search" (*une recherche inquiète*) for the right information. That information is only partially to be found in the genes. Why and how the genetic code is activated, functions, and what the results are, are questions which can only be adequately posed or answered in the context of life, *le vivant*, and experience, *le veçu*.

CONCLUSION

Michel Foucault, in an essay dedicated to Canguilhem, "La vie et la science," characterized a division in French thought between subject-oriented approaches emphasizing meaning and experience and those philosophies which took as their object knowledge, rationality and concepts.[23] The rhetorical effect was marvelous. While everyone had heard of Sartre and Merleau-Ponty, few people beyond a small circle of specialists had actually read the work of Jean Cavaillès on the philosophy of set theory in mathematics or Georges Canguilhem on the history of the reflex arc.[24] The trope was made more tantalizing by allusions to the unflinching and high-stakes activities in the resistance of one side of the pair (Cavaillès was killed by the Nazis after forming a resistance network Canguilhem joined and to which he contributed his medical skills), while the others lived in Paris, writing pamphlets. Foucault was revealing to us a hidden relationship of truth and politics, indicating the figure of another type of intellectual, one for whom totality and authenticity bore different forms and norms.

However, there is a certain insider's humor involved. Twenty years earlier, Canguilhem had employed the same distinctions, awarding them to Jean Cavaillès during the 1930s, while ironizing on those who deduced that a philosophy without a subject must lead to passivity and inaction. Cavaillès, who had made the philosophic journey to Germany during the 1930s and warned early on of the dangers brewing there, did not, Canguilhem tells us, hesi-

tate when the war finally came.[25] Rather than writing a moral treatise to ground his actions, he joined the resistance while finishing,
as best he could, his work on logic. Truth and politics were distinct
domains for these thinkers of the concept: one was ethically
obliged to act in both while never losing site of the specificity of
each of the separate domains. Cavaillès' example of rigorous
thought and principled action, while still a compelling one today
(especially given the misunderstanding and moralism about
French thought rampant across the Rhine, the Channel, and the
Atlantic), would seem to demand a renewed problematization.
The rise and ephemeral glory of structuralism and Althusserianism
have shown that removing the humanist subject in the social sciences by itself guarantees neither an epistemological jump from
ideology to science nor more effective political action (any more
than reinserting a quasi-transcendental subject once again will provide such guarantees). Although Canguilhem's work provides aid
in posing and re-posing such problems, it obviously does not offer
any ready-made answers for the future. Canguilhem has taught us
that deploying ready-made solutions from the past, when history
has moved on, concepts changed, milieus altered, constitutes a
major mistake, one matched in its gravity only by those seeking to
annul history, blur concepts, and equate environments.

NOTES

1. Jean-François Sirinelli, *Génération intellectuelle, Khagneux et Normaliens dans l'entre-deux-guerres* (Paris: Fayard, 1988), p. 465.

2. Ibid., p. 599.

3. *The Normal and the Pathological* (New York: Zone Books, 1989).

4. Jean-Jacques Salomon, "Georges Canguilhem ou la modernité," in *Revue de Métaphysique et de Morale*, no. 1 (Jan.–Mar. 1985).

5. Louis, Althusser, "Présentation," in Pierre Macherey, "La Philosophie de la science de Georges Canguilhem," *La Pensée* 113 (1964): 51.

6. Georges Canguilhem, "Introduction: The Role of Epistemology in Con-
temporary History of Science," in *Ideology and Rationality in the History of the Life Sciences* (Cambridge, Mass.: MIT Press, 1988), p. 9.

7. Ibid., p. 3.

8. Bruno Latour and Geoff Bowker, "A Booming Discipline Short of Discipline: (Social) Studies of Science in France," *Social Studies of Science* 17 (1987).

9. Georges Canguilhem, "L'Objet de l'histoire des sciences," in *Etudes d'histoire et de philosophie des sciences* (Paris: Vrin, 1968; 5th ed., 1983), p .11.

10. Ibid. (1983), p. 16.

11. Ibid., p. 18.

12. Canguilhem's *doctorat d'Etat, La Formation du concept de réflexe aux XVII et XVIII siècles*, was published as a book.

13. François Dagognet, "Une oeuvre en trois temps," *Revue de Metaphysique et de Morale*, no. 1, (1985): 30.

14. Ibid., p. 31.

15. Ibid., p. 37.

16. Georges Canguilhem, "The Question of Normality in the History of Biological Thought," in *Ideology and Rationality in the History of the Life Sciences* (Cambridge, Mass.: MIT Press, 1988; orig. 1973), p. 128.

17. Georges Canguilhem, *The Normal and the Pathological* (New York: Zone Books, 1989; orig.1943), p.131.

18. Ibid., p. 196.

19. Georges Canguilhem, "La Nouvelle connaissance de la vie," in *Etudes d'histoire et de philosophie des sciences* (Paris: Vrin, 1983), p. 335.

20. Dagognet, "Oeuvre," p. 32.

21. "Nouvelle," p. 360.

22. Ibid., p. 362.

23. Michel Foucault, "La vie et la science," *Revue de Métaphysique et de Morale*, no. 1 (1985), translated as "Introduction," in *The Normal and the Pathological* (Zone Books: New York, 1989).

24. Jean Cavaillès, *Méthode axiomatique et formalisme. Essai sur le problème du fondement des mathématiques* (Paris: Hermann, 1938). *Remarques sur la formation de la théorie abstraite des ensembles* (Paris: Hermann, 1939). Georges Canguilhem, *Vie et mort de Jean Cavaillès* (Ambialet: Les Carnets de Baudeser, 1976).

25. Jean Cavaillès, "Protestantisme et Hitlerisme: La crise du Protestantisme allemande," *Esprit*, November 1933.

CHAPTER 5

Artificiality and Enlightenment: From Sociobiology to Biosociality

MICHEL FOUCAULT identified a distinctively modern form of power, "bio-technico-power." Bio-power, he writes, designates "what brought life and its mechanism into the realm of explicit calculations and made knowledge-power an agent of transformation of human life." Historically, practices and discourses of bio-power have clustered around two distinct poles: the "anatomo-politics of the human body," the anchor point and target of disciplinary technologies, on the one hand, and a regulatory pole centered on population with a panoply of strategies concentrating on knowledge, control, and welfare.[1] In this essay I sketch some of the ways in which I believe the two poles of the body and the population are being rearticulated into what could be called a post-disciplinary rationality.[2] My principle focus is the Human Genome Initiative and related developments in biotechnology.[3]

In the annex to his book on Michel Foucault—entitled "On the Death of Man and the Overman"—Gilles Deleuze presents a schema of three "force-forms," to use his jargon, which are roughly equivalent to Michel Foucault's three epistemes. In the Classical form, infinity and perfection are the forces shaping beings; beings have a form toward which they strive and the task of science is to represent correctly the table of those forms in an encyclopedic fashion. In the modern form, finitude establishes a field of life, labor, and language within which Man appears as a distinctive being who is both the subject and object of his own understanding, but an understanding that is never complete because of its very structure. Finally, today in the present, a field of the *surhomme*, or "afterman," in which finitude, as empiricity, gives way to a play of forces and forms that Deleuze labels *fini-illimité*.[4] In this new constellation, beings have neither a perfected form nor an essential opacity. The best example of this "unlimited-finite" is DNA: an infinity of beings can and has arisen from the four bases out of which DNA is constituted. François Jacob, the Nobel Prize-winning biologist, makes a similar point when he writes: "A limited amount of genetic information in the germ line produces an enormous number of protein structures in the soma . . . nature operates to create diversity by endlessly combining bits and pieces."[5] Whether Deleuze has seized the significance of Jacob's facts remains an open question. Still, we must be intrigued when something as cryptic as Rimbaud's formula that "the man of the future will be filled (*chargé*) with animals" takes on a perfectly material meaning, as we shall see when we turn to the concept of model organisms in the new genetics.[6]

Deleuze convincingly claims that Foucault lost his wager that it would be language of the anthropological triad—life, labor, language—that would open the way for a new episteme, washing the figure of Man away like a wave crashing over a drawing in the sand. Foucault himself acknowledged that his prediction had been wrong when, a decade after the publication of *The Order of Things*, he mocked the "relentless theorization of writing," not as the dawning of the new age but as the death rattle of an old one.[7] Deleuze's claim is not that language is irrelevant but rather that the new epochal practices are emerging in the domains of labor and life. Again, whether Deleuze has correctly grasped the significance of these new practices remains to be seen; regardless, they are clearly important. It seems prudent to approach these terms heuristically, taking them singly and as a series of bonded base pairs—labor and life, life and language, language and labor—to see where they lead.

My research strategy focuses on the practices of life as the most potent present site of new knowledges and powers. One logical place to begin an examination of these changes is the American Human Genome Initiative (sponsored by the National Institutes of Health and the Department of Energy) whose mandate is to produce a map of our DNA. The Initiative is very much a techno-science project in two senses. Like most modern science, it is deeply imbricated with technological advances in the most literal way; in this case the confidence that qualitatively more rapid, accurate, and efficient machinery will be invented if the money is made available. (This is already happening.) The second sense of technological is the more important and interesting one: the object to be known—the human genome—will be known in such a way that it can be changed. This dimension is thoroughly modern; one could even say that it instantiates the definition of modern rationality. Representing and intervening, knowledge and power, understanding and reform, are built in, from the start, as simultaneous goals and means.

My initial stance toward the Initiative and its associated institutions and practices is rather traditionally ethnographic: neither committed nor opposed, I seek to describe what is going on. I follow Foucault when he asks, "Shall we try reason? To my mind nothing would be more sterile. First, because the field has nothing to do with guilt or innocence. What we have to do is analyze specific rationalities rather than always invoking the progress of rationalization in general."[8] My ethnographic question is: How will our social and ethical practices change as this project advances? I intend to approach this question on a number of levels and in a variety of sites. First, there is the Initiative itself. Second, there are adjacent enterprises and institutions in which and through which new understandings, new practices, and new technologies of life and labor will certainly be articulated: prime among them the biotechnology industry. Finally, the emergence of bioethics and environmental ethics lodged in a number of different institutions will bear scrutiny as potential reform loci.

THE HUMAN GENOME INITIATIVE

What is the Human Genome Initiative? A genome is "the entire complement of genetic material in the set of chromosomes of a particular organism."[9] DNA is composed of four bases, which bond into two kinds of pairs wound in the famous double helix. The current estimate is that we have about three billion base pairs in our DNA; the mouse has about the same number, while corn or salamanders have more than thirty times as many base pairs in their DNA as we do. No one knows why. Most of the DNA has no known function. It is currently held, not without a certain uneasiness, that 90% of human DNA is "junk." The renowned Cambridge molecular biologist, Sydney Brenner, makes a helpful distinction between "junk" and "garbage." Garbage is something used up and worthless, which one throws away; junk, though, is something one stores for some unspecified future use. It seems highly unlikely that 90% of our DNA is evolutionarily irrelevant, but what its precise relevance could be remains unknown.

Our genes, therefore, constitute the remaining 10% of the DNA. What are genes? They are segments of the DNA that code for proteins. Genes apparently vary in size from about 10,000 base pairs up to two million base pairs. Genes, or at any rate most human genes known today (1% of the presumed total), are not simply spatial units in the sense of a continuous sequence of base pairs; rather, they are regions of DNA made up of spans called "exons," interspersed by regions called "introns." When a gene is activated (and little is known about this process), the segment of DNA is transcribed to a type of RNA. The introns are spliced out, and the exons are joined together to form messenger RNA. This segment is then translated to code for a protein.

We don't know how many genes we have. It is estimated that Homo sapiens has between fifty and one hundred thousand genes—a rather large margin of error. We also don't know where most of these genes are; neither which chromosome they are found on or where they are located on that chromosome. The Initiative is designed to change all this: literally to map our genes. This poses two obvious questions: What is a map? And who is the "our" in "our genes?"

For the first question, then: at present there are three different kinds of maps (linkage, physical, and sequence). Linkage maps are the most familiar to us from the Mendelian genetics we learned in high school. They are based on extensive studies of family genealogies (the Mormon historical archives provide the most complete historical documentation, and the French have a similar project) and show how linked traits are inherited. Linkage maps show which genes are reinherited and roughly where they are on the chromosomes. This provides a helpful first step for identifying the probable location of disease genes in gross terms, but only a first step. In the hunt for the cystic fibrosis gene, for example, linkage maps narrowed down the area to be explored before other types of mapping completed the task.

There are several types of physical maps: "A physical map is a representation of the location of identifiable landmarks on the DNA."[10] The discovery of restriction enzymes provided a major advance in mapping capabilities. These proteins serve to cut DNA into chunks at specific sites. The chunk of DNA can then be cloned and its makeup chemically analyzed and then reconstructed in its original order in the genome. These maps are physical in the literal sense that one has a chunk of DNA and one identifies the gene's location on it, these have been assembled into "libraries." The problem is to locate these physical chunks on a larger chromosomal map. Cloning techniques involving bacteria were used for a number of years, but new techniques, such as "in situ hybridization techniques," are replacing the more time-consuming cloning techniques.

Polymerase chain reaction reduces the need for cloning and physical libraries. It is necessary to clone segments of DNA in order to get enough identical copies to analyze, but this multiplication can now be done more rapidly and efficiently by having the DNA do the work itself, as follows. First, one constructs a small piece of DNA, perhaps 20 base pairs long, called a "primer" or oligonucleotide, which is then commercially made to specification. The raw material from which one takes the base pairs (to be assembled like Lego blocks) is either salmon sperm or the biomass left over from fermentation processes. A particularly rich source is the by-products of soy sauce (hence the Japanese have an edge in this market.) This DNA is refined into single bases, or nucleosides, and recombined according to the desired specifications at a cost of about one dollar per coupling in a DNA synthesizer. The nucleosides could all be made synthetically, but it is currently cheaper given the small quantities needed—most primers are about twenty bases long—to stick to salmon sperm and soy sauce biomass. The current world production of DNA for a year is perhaps several grams, but as demand grows there will be a growing market for the oligonucleotides, custom-made strips of DNA. As Gerald Zon, a biochemist at Applied Biosystems, Inc., put it: the company's dream is to be the world's supplier of synthetic DNA.[11]

Two primers are targeted to attach themselves to the DNA at specific sites called STSs, or sequence-tagged sites. These primers then simply "instruct" the single strand of DNA to reproduce itself without having to be inserted into another organism; this is the polymerase chain reaction. So, instead of having to physically clone a gene, one can simply tell one's friends in Osaka or Omaha which primers to build and where to apply them, and they can do the job themselves (eventually including the DNA preparation, which will be automated). The major advantage of the PCR-STS technique is that it yields information that can be described as "information in a data base: No access to the biological materials that led to the definition or mapping of an STS is required by a scientist wishing to assay a DNA sample for its presence."[12] The computer would tell any laboratory where to look and which primer to construct, and within 24 hours one would have the bit of DNA one is interested in. These segments could then be sequenced by laboratories anywhere in the world and entered into a data base. Such developments have opened the door to what promises to be "a common language for physical mapping of the human genome."[13]

Sequencing means actually identifying the series of base pairs on the physical map. There is ongoing controversy about whether it is necessary to have the complete sequence of the genome (after all, there are vast regions of junk whose role is currently unknown), the complete set of genes (what most genes do is unknown) or merely the sequence of "expressed" genes (i.e., those genes whose protein products are known). While there are formidable technological problems involved in all this, and formidable technological solutions appearing with the predicted rapidity, the principles and the goal are clear enough. "The technical means have become available to root the physical map of the human genome firmly in the DNA sequence itself. Sequence information is the natural language of physical mapping."[14] Of course, the database is not a language but a computer code, and by "natural" our scientist probably means currently most useful.

Still, even when the whole human genome is mapped and even when it is sequenced, as Charles Cantor, Senior Scientist for the Human Genome Initiative for the Department of Energy, has said, we will know nothing about how it works.[15] We will have a kind of structure without function. Much more work remains to be done, and currently is being done, on the hard scientific problems: protein structure, emergent levels of complexity, and the rest. Remember, the entire genetic makeup of human beings is found in most of our cells, but how a cell becomes and remains a brain cell instead of a toe cell is not known. What we will have a decade from now is the material sequence of the *fini-illimitée*, a sequence map of three billion base pairs and between fifty and one hundred thousand genes.

As to the second question: Whose genome is it? Obviously not everyone has exactly the same genes, or junk DNA for that matter; if we did, we would presumably be identical (and probably extinct). There was some debate early on in the project as to exactly whose genome was being mapped; there was a half-serious proposal to have a very rich individual finance the analysis of his own genome.[16] The problem is now shelved, literally, in the clone libraries. The collective standard consists of different physical pieces mapped at centers around the world. Cantor has pointed out that given the way genes are currently located on chromosomes, i.e., linkage maps, the easiest genome to map and sequence would necessarily be composed of the largest number of abnormal genes. In other words, the pathological would be the path to the norm.

Interestingly, all of the sequenced genes need not come from human beings. Genomes of other organisms are also being mapped. Several of these organisms, about which a great deal is already known, have been designated as model systems. Many genes work in the same way, regardless of which living being they are found in. Thus, in principle, wherever we find a specific protein we can know what DNA sequence produced it. This "genetic code" has not changed during evolution and therefore many genes of simpler organisms are basically the same as human genes. Since, for ethical reasons, many simpler organisms are easier to study, much of what we know about human genetics derives from model genetic systems like yeast and mice. Fruit flies have proved to be an extremely useful model system. "One DNA sequence, called the homeo box, was first identified in the genes of fruit flies and later in those of higher organisms, including human beings."[17] This short stretch of nucleotides (in a nearly regular sequence) appears to play a role in turning genes on and off.

Comparisons with even simpler organisms are useful in the identification of genes encoding proteins essential to life. The elaboration of protein sequences and their differences has led to new classifications and a new understanding of evolutionary relationships and processes. An Office of Technology Assessment report laconically asserts the utility of comparisons of human and mouse DNA sequences for the "identification of genes unique to higher organisms because mice genes are more homologous to human genes than are the genes of any other well characterized organism."[18] Hence, today, Rimbaud's premonition of future men "filled with animals" can be made to seem perfectly sound.

FROM STIGMA TO RISK: NORMAL HANDICAPS

My educated guess is that the new genetics will prove to be a greater force for reshaping society and life than was the revolution in physics, because it will be embedded throughout the social fabric at the micro-level by a variety of biopolitical practices and discourses. The new genetics will carry with it its own distinctive promises and dangers.[19] Previous eugenics projects have been modern social projects cast in biological metaphors. Sociobiology, as Marshall Sahlins and so many others have shown, is a social project: from liberal philanthropic interventions designated to moralize and discipline the poor and degenerate; to Rassenhygien and its social extirpations; to entrepreneurial sociobiology and its supply-side social sadism, the construction of society has been at stake.[20]

In the future, the new genetics will cease to be a biological metaphor for modern society and will become instead a circulation network of identity terms and restriction loci, around which and through which a truly new type of autoproduction will emerge, which I call "biosociality." If sociobiology is culture constructed on the basis of a metaphor of nature, then in biosociality nature will be modeled on culture understood as practice. Nature will be known and remade through technique and will finally become artificial, just as culture becomes natural. Were such a project to be brought to fruition, it would stand as the basis for overcoming the nature/culture split.

A crucial step in overcoming the nature/culture split will be the dissolution of the category of "the social." By "society" I don't mean some naturalized universal which is found everywhere and studied by sociologists and anthropologists simply because it is an object waiting to be described: rather I mean something more specific. In *French Modern: Norms and Forms of the Social Environment*, I argue that if our definition is something like Raymond Williams's usage in the first edition of his book of modern commonplaces, *Keywords*, that is, the whole way of life of a people (open to empirical analysis and planned change), then society and the social sciences are the ground plan for modernity.[21] Incidentally, there is no entry for "life" in *Keywords*.

We can see the beginnings of the dissolution of modernist society happening in recent transformations of the concept of risk. Robert Castel, in his 1981 book, *La Gestion des risques*, presents a grid of analysis whose insights extend far beyond his specific concerns with psychiatry, shedding particular light on current trends in the biosciences. Castel's book is an interrogation of postdisciplinary society, which he characterizes thus: first, a mutation of social technologies that minimize direct therapeutic intervention, supplanted by an increasing emphasis on a preventive administrative management of populations at risk; and second, the promotion of working on oneself in a continuous fashion so as to produce an efficient and adaptable subject. These trends lead away from holistic approaches to the subject or social contextualism and move instead toward an instrumentalized approach to both environment and individual as a sum of diverse factors amenable to analysis by specialists. The most salient aspect of this trend for the present discussion is an increasing institutional gap between diagnostics and therapeutics. Although this gap is not a new one, to be sure, the potential for its widening nonetheless poses a new range of social, ethical, and cultural problems, which will become more prominent as biosociality progresses.

Modern prevention is above all the tracking down of risks. Risk is not a result of specific dangers posed by the immediate presence of a person or a group but, rather, the composition of impersonal "factors" which make a risk probable. Prevention, then, is surveillance not of the individual but of likely occurrences of diseases, anomalies, deviant behavior to be minimized, and healthy behavior to be maximized. We are partially moving away from the older face-to-face surveillance of individuals and groups known to be dangerous or ill (for disciplinary or therapeutic purposes), toward projecting risk factors that deconstruct and reconstruct the individual or group subject. This new mode anticipates possible loci of dangerous irruptions, through the identification of sites statistically locatable in relation to norms and means. Through the use of computers, individuals sharing certain traits or sets of traits can be grouped together in a way that not only decontextualizes them from their social environment but also is nonsubjective in a double sense: it is objectively arrived at, and does not apply to a subject in anything like the older sense of the word (that is, the suffering, meaningfully situated, integrator of social, historical, and bodily experiences). Castel names this trend "the technocratic administration of differences." The target is not a person but a population at risk. As an AIDS group in France put it: it is not who one is but what one does that puts you at risk. One's practices are not totalizing, although they may be mortal.[22]

Although epidemiological social-tracking methods were first implemented comprehensively in the tuberculosis campaign, they came to their contemporary maturity elsewhere. The distinction that Castel underscores as symptomatic of this change is that between disease and handicap.[23] A handicap, according to a French government report authored by the highly respected technocrat François Bloch-Lainé, is "any physical, mental or situational condition which produces a weakness or trouble in relation to what is considered normal; normal is defined as the mean of capacities and chances of most individuals in the same society."[24] The concept of handicap was first used officially in England during World War II as a means of evaluating the available workforce in a way that included as many people as possible. Handicaps were deficits to be compensated for socially, psychologically and spatially, not illnesses to be treated: orthopedics not therapeutics. "The concept of handicap naturalizes the subject's history as well as assimilating expected performance levels at a particular historical moment to a naturalized normality."[25] True, this particular individual is blind or deaf or mute or short or tall or paralyzed but can he or she operate the lathe, answer the telephone, guard the door? If not, what can we do to him or her, to the work or to the environment, that would make this possible? Performance is a relative term. Practices make the person; or rather, they don't; they just make practitioners.[26]

There is a large historical step indeed from the rich web of social and personal significations that Western culture inscribed in tuberculosis to the inclusive grid of the welfare state, which has yet to inspire much poetry or yield a celebrated bildungsroman. It has, however, increased life expectancy and produced millions of documents, many of them inscribed in silicon. The objectivism of social factors is now giving way to a new genetics and the beginnings of a redefinition and eventual operationalization of nature.

In a chapter entitled "What Is (Going) to Be Done?" in his book *Proceed with Caution: Predicting Genetic Risk in the Recombinant DNA Era*, Neil A. Holtzman documents the ways that genetic screening will be used in the coming years when its scope and sensitivity are

101

increased dramatically by such technological advances as polymerase chain reaction, which will reduce cost, time, and resistance. There are already tests for such conditions as sickle-cell anemia, and diagnostics for cystic fibrosis and Alzheimer's are on the horizon. These diseases are among the estimated four thousand single-gene disorders. There is a much larger number of diseases, disorders, and discomforts that are polygenetic. Genetic testing will soon be moving into areas in which presymptomatic testing will be at a premium. Thus, Holtzman suggests that once a test is available for identifying a "susceptibility-conferring genotype" for breast cancer, earlier and more frequent mammograms would be recommended or even required (for insurance purposes).[27] He adds: "Monitoring those with genetic predispositions to insulin-dependent diabetes mellitus, colorectal cancer, neurofibromatosis, retinoblastoma, or Wilms tumor for the purpose of detecting early manifestations of the disease might prove beneficial. Discovering those with genetic predispositions could be accomplished either by population-wide screening or, less completely, by testing families in which disease has already occurred."[28] This remark involves a large number of issues, but the only one I will underline here is the likely formation of new group and individual identities and practices arising out of these new truths. There already are, for example, neurofibromatosis groups whose members meet to share their experiences, lobby for their disease, educate their children, redo their home environment, and so on. That is what I mean by biosociality. I am not discussing some hypothetical gene for aggression or altruism. Rather, it is not hard to imagine groups formed around the chromosome 17, locus 16,256, site 654,376 allele variant with a guanine substitution. Such groups will have medical specialists, laboratories, narratives, traditions, and a heavy panoply of pastoral keepers to help them experience, share, intervene, and "understand" their fate.

Fate it will be. It will carry with it no depth. It makes absolutely no sense to seek the meaning of the lack of a guanine base because it has no meaning. One's relation to one's father or mother is not shrouded in the depths of discourse here; the relationship is material even when it is environmental: Did your father smoke? Did your mother take DES? Rest assured they didn't know what they were doing. It follows that other forms of pastoral care will become more prominent in order to overcome the handicap and to prepare for the risks. These therapies for the normal will be diverse, ranging from behavior modifications, to stress management, to interactional therapies of all sorts.[29] We might even see a return of tragedy in post-modernist form, although we will likely not simply rail against the gods, but rather be driven to overcome our fates through more techno-science. The nineties will be the decade of genetics, immunology, and environmentalism; clearly these are the leading vehicles for the infiltration of techno-science, capitalism, and culture into what the moderns call "nature."

Donna Haraway labels these changes "the death of the clinic": "The clinic's methods required bodies and works: we have texts and surfaces. Our dominations don't work by medicalization and normalization any more; they work by networking, communication redesign, stress management."[30] I only partially agree; a multiplication and complex imbrication of rationalities continue to exist. Obviously, older forms of cultural classification of bio-identity such as race, gender, and age have not any more disappeared than medicalization and normalization have, although the meanings and the practices that constitute them certainly are changing. Post-disciplinary practices will co-exist with disciplinary technologies; post social-biological classifications will only gradually colonize older cultural grids. Thus, Troy Duster has shown how testing for sickle-cell anemia has reinforced preexistent racial and social categories even though the distribution of the gene is far wider than the "black" community.[31] In complicated and often insidious ways, the older categories may even take on a renewed force as the new genetics begins to spread not only in the obvious racism so rampant today but more subtly in studies of "blacks," alleged to have higher susceptibility to tuberculosis. My argument is simply that these older cultural classifications will be joined by a vast array of new ones, which will cross-cut, partially supersede, and eventually redefine the older categories in ways which are well worth monitoring.

LABOR AND LIFE

The emergence of modern food, that is, food industrially processed to emphasize uniformity and commoditized as part of an internationalization of world agriculture and distribution, can be dated to the 1870–1914 period.[32] Industrial sugar refining and flour milling for the production of white bread were among the first examples of a constructed consumer need linked to advertising, transportation expansion, a host of processing and preservation techniques, as well as incidentally the rise of modernism in architecture (for example, Buffalo's silos and Minneapolis's grain elevators, as Reyner Banham has shown in his *Concrete Atlantis*).[33] With these changes, agricultural products were on their way to becoming merely an input factor in the production of food, and food was on its way to becoming a "heterogeneous commodity endowed with distinctive properties imparted by processing techniques, product differentiation and merchandising."[34] These processes accelerated during World War I, which here, as in so many other domains, provided the laboratory conditions for inventing, testing, and improving food products on a truly mass scale. Millions of people became accustomed to transformed natural products like evaporated milk as well as new foods like margarine, in which an industrially transformed product substituted for a processed "rural" product, vegetable fats instead of butter. Using methods developed in the textile industry, it was now possible not only to produce foods at industrial levels not constrained by the "natural rhythms" or inherent biological qualities (even if people had bred for these), but even to get people to buy and eat them.

The cultural reaction against foods classified as "artificial" or "processed" was spearheaded in the years between the wars by a variety of lifestyle reformist groups, satirized by George Orwell. Ecological and environmental campaigns, conducted on a national scale by the Nazis with their characteristic vigor, agitated for a return to natural foods (especially whole grain bread), the outlaw of vivisection, the ban of smoking in public places, and the exploration of the effects of environmental toxins on the human genetic material, and so on. Hitler, after all, did not smoke or drink and was a vegetarian.[35] As we have seen in recent decades, not only have the demand for wholesome foods and the obsession with health and environmentalism not meant a return to "traditional" products and processes (although the image of tradition is successfully marketed, few would advocate a return to the real thing with its infected water supplies, low yield, and the like) but it has even accelerated, and will continue to accelerate, the improvement, the enculturization of nature drawing on tradition as a resource to be selectively improved.

Once nature began to be systematically modified to meet industrial and consumer norms—a development perhaps embodied best by the perfect tomato, the right shape, color, size, bred not to break or rot on the way to market, missing only the distinctive taste that dismayed some and pleased others—it could be redescribed and remade to suit other biopolitical specifications like "nutrition." The value of food is now cast not only in terms of how much it imitates whole natural food in freshness and looks but in terms of the health value of its component constituents—vitamins, cholesterol, fiber, salt, and so on. For the first time we have a market in which processed, balanced foods, whose ingredients are chosen in accordance with nutritional or health criteria, can be presented as an alternative superior to nature. Cows are being bred for lower cholesterol, canola for an oil with unsaturated fats: "Once the basic biological requirements of subsistence are met, the 'natural' content of food paradoxically becomes an obstacle to consumption."[36]

Once this cultural redefinition and industrial organization are accepted, then "Nature, whether as land, space, or biological reproduction, no longer poses a binding constraint to the capitalist transformation of the production process and the social division of labor."[37] Bernardo Sorj and his co-authors claim in their *From Farming to Biotechnology* that "the rural labor process is now not so much machine-paced as governed by the capacity of industrial capitals to modify the more fundamental rhythms of biological time."[38] This process leads to increased control over all aspects of the food production process and efforts to make it an industry like any other. New biotechnological techniques working toward the

105

industrial control of plant biology increase the direct manipulation of the nutritional and functional properties of crops, accelerating the trends toward rationalization and the vertical integration of production and marketing required for efficiency. Biotechnological advances like nitrogen fixing or the herbicide resistance of newly engineered plant (and eventually animal) species diminish the importance of land quality and the physicochemical environment as determinants of yields and productivity.

Calgene, a leading California agro-biotech company, based in Davis, is proud of its genetically engineered PGI tomato seeds whose fruit, their 1989 annual report boasted, is superior to a nonengineered control group. Calgene's engineering is no ordinary engineering, though, even by biotech standards; their tomatoes employ an "anti-sense" technique considered to be one of the cutting-edge achievements in the pharmaceutical and therapeutic fields. Anti-sense involves disrupting the genetic message of a gene by interfering with either the synthesis of messenger RNA or its expression, that is, before its instructions to make a protein are carried out. While the concept is simple, developing techniques that are refined and specific enough to achieve the desired results is not. Field trials, according to the annual report, "verified the ability of Calgene's antisense (AS-1) gene to reduce fruit rotting while increasing total solid content, viscosity and consistency."[39] The gene significantly reduces the expression of an enzyme that causes the breakdown of pectin in fruit cell walls and thereby decreases the shelf life. "This new technology provides a natural alternative to artificial processing, which means that the tomatoes delivered to consumers in the future promise to be closer to homegrown in firmness, color and taste."[40] It looks good, it travels well, and it may soon taste like what those who have still eaten traditional tomatoes think they should taste like.

Traditional tastes pose a challenge not a threat to technoscience; the more one specifies what is missing from the new product, the more the civilizing process proceeds.[41] Tomatoes aren't what they used to be? But you don't like bugs either? Let's see what can be done. A company in Menlo Park is perfecting a bioengineered vanillin, one of the most complex of smells and tastes.

Scientists are approaching museums armed with the PCR technique, which enables them to take a small piece of DNA and amplify it millions of times.[42] This recovered DNA could then, at least in principle, be reintroduced into contemporary products. If eighteenth century tomatoes are your fancy, there is no reason a priori why one day a boutique biotech company aiming at the Berkeley or Cambridge market couldn't produce one that is consistently pesticide resistant, transportable, and delicious for you—and those just like you. In sum, the new knowledges have already begun to modify labor practices and life processes in what Enlightenment botanists called nature's second kingdom.[43]

IN PRAISE OF ARTIFICIALITY

What are we to make of all this? Before rushing to judgment it seems wisest first to proceed with both caution and *élan* in attempting to pose questions in a heuristic fashion. François Dagonet and Donna Haraway see a potentially epochal opportunity extending beyond the dreary march of instrumentalization and objectification (although it is that as well). They see present today a Nietzschean potential to free us from some of our longest lies.

François Dagognet, a prolific and fascinating French philosopher of the sciences, a materialist in the style of the eighteenth century—a recent book is in praise of plastics, but he has also written on the extraordinary diversity of leaf forms—identifies three major revolutions in our attitudes toward the world. The first was the possibility of a mechanization of the world, associated with Galileo. The second was the French Revolution, which showed humanity that its institutions were its own and that consequently men could become "masters of the social tie." The third, which is now within our will, concerns neither the universe nor society but life itself.[44]

For Dagognet the main obstacle to the full exploration and exploitation of life's potentials is a residual naturalism. He traces the roots of "naturalism" to the Greeks. The artisan or artist, it was held, imitates that which is nature. Although man works on nature, he doesn't change it ontologically because human productions never contain an internal principle of generation.[45] This naturalism has endured. From the Greeks to the present, a variety of naturalisms have held to the following axioms: (1) the artificial is never as good as the natural; (2) generation furnishes the proof of life (life is auto-production); (3) homeostasis (auto-regulation) is the golden rule.[46] Contemporary normative judgments continue to affirm the superiority of the biological, the insecurity of human works, the risks linked to artificiality and the certitude that the initial situation—the Golden Pond or the Sierra—was incomparably better.

Dagognet argues that nature has not been natural, in the sense of pure and untouched by human works, for millennia. More provocatively, he asserts that nature's malleability offers an "invitation" to the artificial. Nature is a blind *bricoleur*, an elementary logic of combinations, yielding an infinity of potential differences. These differences are not prefigured by final causes, and there is no latent perfection seeking homeostasis. If the word "nature" is to retain a meaning, it must signify an uninhibited polyphenomenality of display. Once understood in this way, the only natural thing for man to do would be to facilitate, encourage, accelerate its unfurling: thematic variation, not rigor mortis. Dagognet challenges us in a consummately modern fashion: "Either we go toward a sort of veneration before the immensity of 'that which is' or one accepts the possibility of manipulation."

Donna Haraway concludes her iconoclastic and enlightened 1985 "Manifesto for Cyborgs" by arguing that "taking responsibility for the social relations of science and technology means refusing an anti-science metaphysics, a demonology of technology, and so means embracing the skillful task of reconstructing the boundaries of daily life, in partial connection with others, in communication with all of our parts." She applauds the subversion of "myriad organic wholes (e.g., the poem, the primitive culture, the biological organism)" and proclaims that "the certainty of what counts as nature—a source of insight and a promise of innocence—is undermined, perhaps fatally."[47]

As with nature, so too, it seems, with culture.

NOTES

1. Michel Foucault, *The History of Sexuality, vol. 1: An Introduction* (New York: Pantheon Books, 1978), p. 139. Special thanks to Vincent Sarich, Jenny Gumperz, Frank Rothchild, Guy Micco, Hubert Dreyfus, and Thomas White.

2. I don't think postdisciplinary can be equated with postmodern.

3. *Mapping Our Genes, Genome Projects: How Big, How Fast?* (Washington, D.C.: Office of Technology Assessment, 1988).

4. Gilles Deleuze, *Foucault* (Paris: Editions du Minuit, 1986), p. 140. Foucault's version is found in *The Order of Things: An Archaelogy of the Human Sciences* (New York: Vintage Books, 1966). On natural history in the classical age, see Henri Daudin, *Cuvier et Lamarck: Les Classes zoologiques et l'idée de série animale* (Paris: Librairie Felix Alcan, 1926). On the philosophic understanding of Man, see Jules Vuillemin, *L'Heritage kantien et la revolution copernicienne: Fichte, Cohen, Heidegger* (Paris: P.U.F., 1954).

5. François Jacob, *The Possible and the Actual* (New York: Pantheon Books, 1982), p. 39.

6. Deleuze, *Foucault*, "L'homme de l'avenir est chargé des animaux," p. 141.

7. Michel Foucault, "Truth and Power," in *Power/Knowledge*, ed. Colin Gordon (New York: Pantheon Books, 1980), p. 127; idem, *The Order of Things: An Archaelogy of the Human Sciences* (New York: Random House, 1970; orig. 1966), p. 387.

"For Classical thought, Man does not occupy a place in nature through the intermediary of the limited, regional, specific 'nature' that is granted to him, as to all other beings as a birthright. If human nature is interwoven with nature, it is by the mechanisms of knowledge and by their functioning; or rather in the general mechanisms of the Classical episteme, nature, or human nature, and their relations, are definite and predictable functional relations. And Man, as a primary reality with his own density, as the difficult object and soverign subject of all possible knowledge, has no place in it" (*Order of Things*, p. 310).

8. Michel Foucault, "The Subject and Power," in H. Dreyfus and P. Rabinow, *Michel Foucault Beyond Structuralism and Hermeneutics* (Chicago: University of Chicago Press, 1983), p. 210.

9. *Mapping Our Genes*, p. 21.

10. Ibid., p. 30.

11. Interview, March 19, 1990.

12. Maynard Olson, Leroy Hood, Charles Cantor, and David Botstein. "A Common Language for Physical Mapping of the Human Genome," *Science* 245 (September 29, 1989).

13. Ibid., p. 1434.

14. Ibid., p. 1435. Natural languages exist in a context of culture and background practices. Codes are representational but only in the "representation degree zero" sense of transparency and definitional arbitrariness. I intend to deal with "language" and its relations with "labor" and "life" in another paper.

15. Charles Cantor, "Opening Remarks," at Human Genome: I, San Diego, October 1, 1989.

16. If, as Allan Wilson and his team convincingly argue, there was an "original Eve," the mother of us all, in Africa about 200,000 years ago, there would be an argument to take an African genome as the standard from which other groups have varied. A. C. Wilson, E. A. Zimmer, E. M. Prager, T. D. Kocher, "Restriction mapping in the molecular systematics of mammels: A restrospective salute," in B. Fernholm, K. Bremer, and H. Jornvall, eds., *The Hierarchy of Life* (Amsterdam: Elsevier Publishing), pp. 407–19.

17. *Mapping the Human Genome*, p. 67.

18. Ibid., p. 68.

19. Daniel Kevles and John Heilbron both agreed with the importance of the social impact of the Initiative. Heilbron: "Oh, a thousand times more important." February 14, 1990.

20. Marshall Sahlins, *The Use and Abuse of Biology: An Anthropological Critique of Sociobiology* (Ann Arbor: University of Michigan Press, 1976). Robert N. Proctor, *Racial Hygiene: Medicine under the Nazis* (Cambridge, Mass.: Harvard University Press, 1988). Daniel J. Kevles, *In the Name of Eugenics: Genetics and the Uses of Human Heredity* (Berkeley: University of California Press, 1985). Benno Muller-Hill, *Murderous Science: Elimination by Scientific Selection of Jews, Gypsies, and Others: Germany, 1933–45* (Oxford: Oxford University Press, 1988).

21. Paul Rabinow, *French Modern: Norms and Forms of the Social Environment* (Chicago: University of Chicago, 1995; orig. 1989).

22. The third term here is genetics. If, as is hinted at, there were a genetic component to AIDS susceptibility, then the equation would be more complex.

23. Robert Castel, *La Gestion des risques, de l'anti-psychiatrie à l'apres-psychanalyse* (Paris: Les Editions du Minuit, 1981).

24. François Bloch-Lainé, *Etude du problème général de l'inadaptation des personnes handicapées* (La Documentation française, 1969), p.111, cited in Castel, *La Gestion*, p. 117.

25. Castel, *La Gestion*, p. 122.

26. Credit is due to James Faubion for clarity on this point.

27. Tom White rightly underlines that all of these developments could and most likely will be contested.

28. Neil A. Holtzman, *Proceed with Caution: Genetic Testing in the Recombinant DNA Era* (Baltimore and London: Johns Hopkins University Press, 1989), pp. 235–36.

29. Robert Castel, *Advanced Psychiatric Society* (Berkeley: University of California Press, 1986).

30. Donna Haraway, "A Manifesto for Cyborgs," *Socialist Review* 15, no. 2 (March-April 1985): 69.

31. Troy Duster, *Backdoor to Eugenics* (London: Routledge, 1990).

32. A fuller treatment would have to deal with both domestication and agri-

culture in evolutionary perspective. Thanks to Tom White for discussions on this and other points.

33. Reyner Banham, *A Concrete Atlantis: U.S. Industrial Building and European Modern Architecture 1900–1925* (Cambridge, Mass: MIT Press, 1986).

34. David Goodman, Bernardo Sorj, and John Wilkinson, *From Farming to Biotechnology: A Theory of Agro-Industrial Development* (Oxford: Basil Blackwell, 1987), p. 60.

35. A good summary can be found in Proctor's *Racial Hygiene*, chapter 8, "The 'Organic Vision' of Nazi Racial Science."

36. Ibid., p. 193.

37. Ibid., p. 58.

38. Goodman et al., *From Farming to Biotechnology*, p. 47.

39. *Planning for the Future* (Calgene 1989 Annual Report), p. 14.

40. Ibid.

41. Keith Thomas, *Man and the Natural World: A History of the Modern Sensibility* (New York: Pantheon Books, 1983).

42. Norman Arnheim, Tom White, and William E. Rainey, "Application of PCR: Organismal and Population Biology," *BioScience* 40, no. 3 (1987): 174–83.

43. François Delaporte, *Nature's Second Kingdom* (Cambridge, Mass: MIT Press, 1982; orig.1979)

44. François Dagognet, *La Maîtrise du vivant* (Paris: Hachette, 1988) p. 41.

45. In his *Generation des animaux*, Aristotle gives the processes of generation the key role among living beings (self-production of one's self). "Man is born of man but a bed is not born from a bed."

46. Dagonet, p. 41.

47. Haraway, "Manifesto," p. 41.

CHAPTER 6

Galton's Regret:
Of Types and Individuals

> We read of the dead body of Jezebel being
> devoured by the dogs of Jezreel, so that no man
> might say, "This is Jezebel," and that the dogs left
> only her skull, the palms of her hands, and the
> soles of her feet; but the palms of the hands
> and the soles of the feet are the very remains by
> which a corpse might be most surely identified,
> if impressions of them, made during life,
> were available.
>
> (Sir Francis Galton)

SIR FRANCIS GALTON (1892) began his book on fingerprinting with the first of a long series of Victorian commonplaces: how modern science has distinguished the truth from appearance. Of the two kinds of marks on the hands and soles of the feet, one offered false hope and the other true clues. The creases of the palms, to which a great deal of significance had been attributed over the centuries and across cultures, revealed no real secrets. Their patterns literally embodied only the sheerest physical index of use, labor, or leisure. Palm prints, for Galton, did indicate something about the individual's experience and station in life but not enough to provide a means of identification to sort individual from individual, only class from class. On the other hand, the so-called papillary ridges were the most crucial anthropological data. These ridges, Galton concluded, offered the surest source of individual identification precisely because they were, for reasons unknown, distinctive to each person and remained identical throughout life. "There is no prejudice to be overcome in procuring these most trustworthy sign-manuals, no vanity to be pacified, no untruths to be guarded against" (Galton 1892). Although they revealed nothing about experience, they were indelible marks of individuality.

According to Galton, the first scientific documentation, as opposed to the unscientific use in many cultures, of the systematicity and hence usefulness of fingerprints for identification purposes was carried out in 1923 by Dr. Purkenje of the University of Breslau. The first practical usage of fingerprinting took place in Bengal. As a Major Ferris of the India Staff Corps put it, "The uniformity in the colour of the hair, eyes and complexion of the Indian races renders identification far from easy." The proverbial "prevalence of unveracity" of the Oriental races provided the motivation for these gentlemen to perfect a reliable identification system, one whose basis lay in a marker beyond or below the cunning will of native or criminal. These colonial officers had stumbled across a "sign-manual that differentiates the person who made it, throughout the whole of his life, from all the rest of mankind" (Galton 1892). Physiological research demonstrated that a distinctive pattern developed as early as the fourth month of pregnancy and was fully formed by the sixth month. Although through use or injury the shape of the fingertip did change, the number of the ridges and their minutiae, which compose the pattern, did not. Galton demonstrated that identification could usually be shown with just five elements. Once a system was set in place to photograph the prints acquired through simple inking methods, little skill was necessary to obtain fingerprints and not much more to interpret them.

During the 1880s, the reigning system of criminal identification was in a positivistic sense much more scientific. Alphonse Bertillon had developed a system of twelve anthropomorphic measures (head length, head breadth, middle finger length, foot length, length and breadth of the ear, height of the bust, eye color, etc.). These elements yielded almost a million possible combinations, easily increased to infinity with the addition of a few more variables when necessary. "Bertillonage" was performed by three operators and three clerks during an examination taking 6–8 minutes. Data were entered via a code on cards, which were then photographed, making it easy to reproduce them for distribution to other identification centers (courts and prisons). The French state gave Bertillon's system official status in 1883. Galton had gone to France to witness the use of Bertillonage directly and was impressed with the analytic methods as well as their institutional implementation. In his book, Galton acknowledged the comprehensive scope of Bertillon's measurements but insisted that fingerprinting was more certain. "Bertillonage can rarely supply more than grounds for very strong suspicion: the method of finger prints affords certainty. . . . Let us not forget two great and peculiar methods of finger prints: they are self-signatures, free from all possibility of faults in observation or of clerical error; and they apply throughout life" (Galton 1892).

This essay is not the place to rehearse the decline and fall of nineteenth-century physical anthropology's dependence on phenotypic measurements (Gould 1981; Nye 1984; Wechsler 1982). Although Galton triumphed over Bertillon's system, I introduce the latter because many of its analytic strategies, thoroughly transformed a century later through the use of entirely different genetic and molecular biological techniques (i.e., measurement, distribution, comparison, and statistical evaluation) are the subject matter of the following sections.

Sir Francis Galton was frankly not entirely satisfied with fingerprints as a means of identification. Although they did provide a powerful device for the identification of criminals (and everyone else, for that matter), they revealed nothing about individual character or group affiliation. After examining prints from English, Welsh, Jews, Negroes, and Basques, Galton bowed to his results; there was an identical range and frequency of fingerprint elements and types. Analysis of the prints of artists, scientists, and idiots revealed no systematic differences. Galton admitted that he had "great expectations, that have been falsified, namely, their use in indicating Race and Temperament" (Galton 1892). He was forced to conclude, not without a certain regret, "Consequently *genera* and species are here seen to be formed without the slightest aid from either Natural or Sexual Selection." Fingerprints were individual, yet bore no trace of character, society, or evolution, and to that extent, constituted for the Victorian founder of eugenics a major disappointment.

Galton's methods were revised in 1897 and that system is still in use worldwide today (Fincher 1989). Obviously, the story of fingerprinting's triumph over rival identification methods has a more complicated institutional and juridical history, which remains to be written. During the 1970s and 1980s, laser technology has enabled forensic experts to make increasingly precise prints from minimal traces; vastly more powerful computers have made the system more efficient by allowing rapid comparison searches, which earlier would have taken years. Regional computer networks have been put in place. The basic principles of fingerprinting, however, have not changed—Galton's regret remains.

THE FRYE TEST

Considering how important science and technology have been in America since its inception, the legal precedents upon which the admissibility of scientific expertise have rested in the American legal system are surprisingly tardy and thin. As opposed to patent law, which was laid down in the early days of the republic and continues to inform the legal context in which contemporary inventions such as recombinant DNA methods and processes are adjudicated, it was only in 1923 that general legal principles were formulated for the admissibility of scientific evidence. This judicial threshold was crossed in the Frye decision, in which it was held that a precursor of the polygraph test was not admissible as evidence in a murder trial. Of more lasting importance than the specific decision itself were the standards that the court proposed for admitting scientific expertise into the courtroom. The Court of Appeals for the District of Columbia held, "Just when a scientific principle or discovery crosses the line between the experimental and demonstrable stages is difficult to define. Somewhere in this twilight zone the evidential force of principle must be recognized and while courts will go a long way in admitting expert testimony deduced from a well recognized scientific principle or

115

discovery, the thing from which the deduction is made must be sufficiently established to have gained general acceptance in the particular field in which it belongs" (Neufeld 1989). Although the court cited no precedent, its own decision established the precedent to which the contemporary debates still defer. The points at issue are (1) identifying the appropriate scientific field or fields; (2) quantifying "general acceptance" in the particular field; (3) deciding whether proof of validity of "the thing from which the deduction is made" must support the underlying scientific theory or the technique or perhaps both. These criteria seemed to have received little or no criticism, either legal, technical, or cultural, in the decades following the Frye decision. Fingerprinting, as well as improved polygraphs and other such devices, was used widely by local and national law enforcement agencies and routinely accepted into evidence by the courts. Because this broad acceptance must have had echoes and anchors in the broader social arena, it would be illuminating to trace the development of the popular image of the police laboratory during the interwar and immediate postwar periods. These were decades, it seems, in which the law, science and the public representations of the truth were made to harmonize.

An example of the reexamination and devastating criticism of previously unchallenged truths can be seen in the diphenylamine or "paraffin" test used to detect gunshot residue on the hands. The procedure was introduced in the early 1930s and admitted as valid by the courts in 1936, even though an official FBI evaluation of 1935 questioned its authoritativeness. It was not until 1967 that a comprehensive independent study evaluated the evidence and showed the test's unreliability. "Among the substances that also gave a positive test result and could easily be found in residue form on anyone's hand were evaporated urine, tobacco ash, various pharmaceuticals and colored finger nail polish" (Neufeld 1989). The paraffin test met the Frye standard of "general acceptability" for 30 years and had been used widely. It was not until the mid-1970s that a federal policy on evidence was formulated. Most surprising of all, it was not until the late 1980s, with the introduction of the so-called DNA fingerprinting, that sustained debate about how unclear the standards of scientific expertise really are unfolded.

As did so many other aspects of American society and culture, forensic institutions and procedures for establishing truth began to change in the mid-1960s, one of those periodic conjunctures of accelerated modernization of law, technology, and public opinion in the United States. The institution that embodies this modernization is the Law Enforcement Assistance Administration (LEAA), created in 1968 as part of the Omnibus Crime Control and Safe Streets Act. Supreme Court decisions strengthening defendants' rights explicitly hastened the search for technical and scientific evidence. The authority of both FBI and local police in general, as well as their taken-for-granted procedures of obtaining evidence and using it, was under attack. Although the long-range conservative response to this situation was to change those interpreting the law, in the short run technological responses were accelerated as a means of establishing more convincing types of evidence, especially evidence not dependent on confession. As early as 1966, the California Supreme Court drew an important Fifth Amendment distinction between communicative or testimonial evidence, which is subject to privilege against self-incrimination, and physical or real evidence, which is not protected. The court noted that the privilege "offers no protection against compulsion to submit to fingerprinting, photographing, or measurements, to write or speak for identification, to appear in court, to stand, to assume a stance, to walk, or to make a particular gesture" (OTA 1990).

The Crime Laboratory Proficiency Testing Program initiated by LEAA concluded that many laboratories were below par. The response to this amateurism was unambiguous: update and expand. More than half of the nation's crime laboratories came into existence after 1970, many through funding from the LEAA. Its presence accelerated the search for new technologies in the criminology area, including work on bloodstains, trace metal detection, and voice detection (Gianelli 1980). The modernization of forensics followed the analysis of the sociological literature on professionalization extremely well. As expected, one saw the differentiation of specialists and technicians, the formalization and

117

jargonization of standards and practices, government regulation and the like.

The first major reevaluation of the Frye principles came in challenges to voice print technology, a new device developed by police crime laboratory technicians in Michigan. This technology imitated fingerprinting to identify a person on basically unalterable phenotypical characteristics. Just as each individual has a unique set of fingerprints, so too, perhaps, each individual has a unique voice. A technique called "sound spectroscopy" was developed, which produced an abstract printed patter—a voice print—from a tape recording. When the scientific basis of the technique was challenged in court, the first question to be answered, following the Frye principles, was, since there was no preexisting scientific voice print research community, who were the appropriate scientific experts? Were they the inventors of sound spectroscopy, the Michigan State Police? Or did the identification of voice patterns fall into a wider series of specialties including anatomy, physiology, physics, psychology, and linguistics? Not only did the inventors of the technique appear to have a conflict of interest, but they were mere laboratory technicians, not scientists with advanced degrees.

Under the auspices of LEAA, a national commission was formed to resolve the issue. The main point to be decided was simple: Were there scientific grounds to believe that speech contained a hidden pattern which could be used to identify a particular individual, and, if so, did the sound spectrography technique adequately capture this particularity? Although the experts all agreed that there were regularities, no definitive elements or patterns could be identified; there was simply too much variation both among individuals and within an individual's own speech patterns. Again in typical reformist bureaucratic fashion, the committee did not close the case but called for a program of research and development leading to a science-based technology of voice identification. Although itself in many ways a technological throwback to an earlier era, voice printing nonetheless raised a series of interpretive issues arising from the Frye precedents. Who is the community of experts? What constitutes independent verification?

What is the role of national agencies? These institutional issues remain open in contemporary debates about DNA methods: What should the relationship be between the businesses who perform the tests, the FBI, the academic community? Should there be impartial national commissions to set standards? How reliable are laboratory procedures? Which studies need to be done?

Although these institutional issues demonstrate continuity in framing the legal and bureaucratic dimensions of establishing truth, I believe an important turning point was reached in the voice print controversy. Embedded in the National Commission's deliberations was a partial response to Galton's regret. The commission opined about an evolving science of voice identification, but, in fact, there was no evolving science of voice identification because it was not a science. Historically, failure of reform movements with their dubious claims to science have frequently resulted in more funding to improve the science. The susceptibility to voluntary control is an old theme stemming from the older moralistic disciplines of the nineteenth century, echoes of which are still found in the Frye decision's statement that individuals have an involuntary propensity to tell the truth. Along with these older strata was something not exactly new in itself (population genetics, after all, had been in existence for close to a century) but whose conceptual migration into forensics would be catapulted onto center stage by developments in recombinant DNA technology, the necessary *linking of the individual to a population*.

The invention of electrophoretic bloodstain analysis, in the early 1980s, provides an example of the crossing of this new threshold. Unlike voice printing, electrophoretic bloodstain analysis was a technique developed for entirely different purposes and then adapted for forensic uses. It entered into the court system as early as 1978, but the majority of precedent-setting decisions concerning its admissibility as evidence took place in the mid-1980s. The courts proceeded from the voice printing debate foregrounding questions of credentials and professionalization, weighing conflicting claims of authority over content, e.g., do results have to appear in peer-reviewed scientific journals to count as fact (Harmon 1989)? This attention to authority, procedure,

119

and precedent, although appropriate in the logic of legal proof, tended to obscure qualitative differences in these technologies from older ones.

DNA typing differs qualitatively from "the evolving science of voice identification." This claim obviously does not imply that procedures based on valid principles should carry automatic acceptance in individual cases, because technical mistakes and simple human errors like mislabeling samples are made all the time. Furthermore, it is the nature of an adversarial legal system for partisan interpretation to be presented tactically. According to Peter Neufeld, as of 1989, electrophoretic bloodstain evidence had been introduced in approximately 500 court cases in New York. The defense challenged expert witnesses only twice with other expert witnesses. In both instances, following Frye hearings, the trial courts decided to exclude the serological evidence. "What does this result say about the quality of justice in the other 498 cases?" (Neufeld 1989). It means unequal access to technology emerges as a critical issue in a period of technological change. Scientific illiteracy of the judiciary, legal profession, and the public will be best protected against through education and adversarial proceedings.

MODERNIZING STANDARDS: FBI AND POPULATION

The FBI entered the field of DNA technology in late 1984 with a collaborative project with the National Institutes of Health. By 1986, agents were visiting laboratories in both England and the United States to survey and learn cutting-edge technologies. Private industry, government, and the university world cooperated eagerly. In July 1987, an evaluation was made that the technology held great potential, and a decision was taken to establish an FBI research team at Quantico, Virginia (Hicks 1989). The center was staffed by specialists versed in traditional blood-grouping and protein-testing methods. The University of Virginia cooperated by organizing a course in molecular genetics for the agents. The FBI sees itself playing a catalyst role for streamlining, improving, and making these technologies more reliable and cost-effective. To this end, it holds training sessions for state and local officials. A visiting scientist program at the bureau's Forensic Science Research and Training Center enables local forensic technicians from across the country to return home fully trained and prepared to set up labs.

At the heart of the FBI's efforts is the issue of standardization. Having decided that the technology works, the FBI understood that without relatively standardized procedures and (even more importantly) without the prospect of a normative database, the future impact of this technology would be limited. As John W. Hicks told the assembled experts at the Banbury Center of Cold Spring Harbor Laboratory, "There must be uniformity within the crime laboratory community on the DNA test methods used so that the profiles developed can be effectively cataloged and compared. There have already been some discussions within the forensic community exploring the feasibility of DNA data banks and uniform test protocols" (Hicks 1989). This call for norms involves more than cost-effectiveness or state control, although features of each are present. The need for norms derives from the nature of the project: without an adequate database for the population genetics, identification of individuals could only be exclusionary at a relatively low level. As two other authors in the Banbury volume put it: "A number of organizations around the world are now considering development of large data bases containing DNA profiles of all individuals in specific populations. As the application of this technology continues to expand there is a growing concern as to whether standardization of systems is necessary" (Rose and Keith 1989). The answer is yes.

Of course, there will be problems to iron out. Enforcing a common standard is never easy, particularly in a field in which private companies are doing the bulk of the analysis and want to retain proprietary rights over their techniques. In the general spirit of cooperation that currently marks these encounters, one participant suggested "an alternative approach that might satisfy the need for global compatibility could be the use of a completely standardized core system by all laboratories interested in interact-

121

ing with a large data base, along with any additional systems the individual laboratories might choose to use" (Rose and Keith 1989). This approach would protect the proprietary rights of the companies involved while enriching the database from which probabilities are derived. The FBI advocates imitating the regionalization approach adopted by state officials running newborn screening programs. Not only does regionalization permit regulation of the procedures employed, it is also cost-effective and most easily meets the demands of the congressional oversight committee that blind screening be included as a control.

The FBI is explicitly seeking to reassure civil libertarians. The information included in the database would be chosen in such a manner that it could not be used abusively. Citing their choice of Jeffrey's variable number of tandem repeats (VNTR) approach, an FBI spokesman argues, "There is no known relationship between these numbers and any physical or mental condition. Selection of the genetic markers in the data base will be made with an eye to eliminating the potential interest of the data to the private sector. Probes will not be used that are linked to disease conditions or personality traits" (Kearney 1990). Although the genetic arbitrariness of the approach is meant to reassure, it does contain some ambiguities. The very reason the data are chosen—their very arbitrariness—opens up avenues for other arbitrary correlations, ones that might assign a meaning function to them or interpret them as a marker of other conditions. Eric Lander cautions that we might well see random correlations being run: "The allele, at this locus about what I know nothing, tends to come up in rapists" (Lander in Ballantyne et al. 1989). This is not an idle fantasy. We also read, "The individuals who commit violent crimes are often repeat offenders" (Kirby 1990) and "Several states are considering collecting DNA identification profiles of certain categories of repeat offenders" (Hicks 1989). Risk profile analysis, moving beyond socioeconomic variables, might well be hard to resist. The most obvious means of preventing such abuses would be to simply destroy the DNA upon which the tests were done; defense attorneys, however, might well resist this move because it denies them the possibility of verifying the analyses.

If risk correlations for their own sake are one danger, another is to find a more than correlational meaning to the data one has. Alec Jeffreys cautions against assuming that "the regions most of us who are using this technique are looking at are noncoding. I am not aware of any formal proof that any of these regions is a noncoding region. There are examples showing that some of these regions are coding and that they are probably all coding" (Jeffreys in Ballantyne et al. 1989, p. 36). Jeffreys' point is a general and recurring one and carries with it a caution that might be phrased as follows: although a great deal is being discovered, very little is yet understood. The effort to understand will no doubt follow the data being discovered.

WHY DNA FINGERPRINTING IS REALLY DNA TYPING

Eric Lander interrupted a forensic expert's summary, "In forensic analysis, basically we compare the questioned sample with a known sample, side by side. It does not matter whether it is a voice screen, an infrared spectra, a GC chromotagram, or DNA; if they show identical patterns. . . ," by asking, "Are they the same person?" "No," the expert responded, "the same pattern." Another expert added, "I do not think we are talking about unique identification. We are talking about things from profiles with some statistical evidence for a percentage of the population that may carry an array of types, and we are putting a value on them so that some people can properly evaluate what they mean" (Lander in Ballantyne et al. 1989). DNA forensics is a question of *types*. The conceptual foundations of the typing methodology are uncontested, although the current technology will no doubt soon appear quaint.

With the population data, there are both factual and interpretation problems outstanding. The presence or absence of a polymorphism can exclude with absolute certainty. A suspect with one blood group cannot be responsible for a bloodstain from another blood group. However, inclusion depends on population genetics and, hence, on probabilities. Eric Lander points out that although there may be as many as three million sites of DNA variation between individuals, only three or four restriction-fragment-length-polymorphisms (RFLP) have been used in forensics. Grant that the various technical problems of proper laboratory work and overcoming degraded or insufficient samples have been solved, the main question mark for the RFLP approach to forensic identification is population genetics. The basic theory of population genetics has been established for a century now and its mathematics for half a century. However, neither the stakes nor the standards relevant to estimating the growth of a turtle population over centuries and the guilt or innocence of one human individual are yet commensurate.

Lander provides a succinct outline of the relevant principles. Assume that the DNA sample from the suspect matches that found at the crime, i.e., the RFLP lengths are the same on the radiograph. The question is, How likely is it that this match is a random one? The only way to answer the question is through population genetics. If we knew the distribution of the RFLP we would know the answer. Such data exist today only for very small samples. It follows that the more loci one used, the higher the odds of a specific determination would be; therefore, multiply the probes. The concept is straightforward; empirically, there are often problems. First, has the correct population been identified? It was shown as early as 1918, during the First World War, that populations vary significantly by blood type. A great deal of work has been done since to detail this variation. The explanation for variation is genetic drift, e.g., Tay-Sachs disease is found with a great frequency among East European Jews, a formerly relatively isolated population.

Hypervariable loci are the best markers to use if one is seeking to differentiate populations. The study of this type of variation was modernized—standardized, operationalized, commercialized—by international studies of HLA genes, which control transplant rejection (among other things). There is a large database for HLA variation. Variation is significant, e.g., the frequency of one HLA gene is 0.2% in Japanese and 19% in French Caucasians. Thus, a Frenchman would be 9025 times more likely to be a homozygote for HLA-A1 than a Japanese would be. This range of variation has been found for other alleles. However, it is important to specify between which groups variation is being studied and that these groups are true groups in terms of population genetics criteria. Thus, do Puerto Ricans and Mexicans (Hispanic) really belong in the same category; do Russians and Italians (Caucasian)? Whatever the politics of classification was to establish the system of categories (Caucasian, Black, Asian, Native American, Hispanic), the categories are clearly too broad for accurate forensic population genetics.

A second problem is whether the sample is large enough that the observed frequencies accurately represent the true population frequencies. Statistical techniques exist to correct for nonrandom sampling, but they have not always been applied in forensics. More care in definition and selection and bigger samples must be introduced. Even with large numbers, it is not always easy to establish whether the sample is random or not. This is a serious problem. As Lander says, "Were it not unethical and unconstitutional, a court might compel randomly chosen individuals to provide blood samples in a population survey" (Lander 1989). He suggests the norm of standards used in political polling: a replaceable, detailed, anonymous survey checked against census data.

A third problem is whether each locus is in Hardy-Weinberg equilibrium and the loci are together in linkage equilibrium. This requirement is pertinent because it is the premise on which the calculations for randomness in a population depend. The HLA frequencies appear to be in Hardy-Weinberg equilibrium. The lack of Hardy-Weinberg equilibrium poses a problem for VNTR data. Not surprisingly, "free interbreeding" appears not to be the American norm. We have ethnic and religious subgroups. Lander reiterates that results indicative of nonequilibrium do not invalidate the laws of population genetics and Mendelian inheritance. They reveal our inadequate understanding of the American population. This problem can be corrected through more studies and better statistical procedures. Another expert concurs that the issues will be resolved only "when the data bases are sufficiently expanded to provide large enough sample numbers to verify or reject the usual statistical approaches used" (Putterman 1990). The FBI is planning to undertake large sampling studies as a means of refining categories.

A Modest Proposal

To ensure adequate statistical protections, more finely drawn groups will have to be included in the database. Because it is currently in bad taste to refer directly to races or breeding populations, various subsets of this data pool will be called ethnic. Of course, these ethnic groups will be measured on a common grid so that individuals can be placed in populations and subpopulations related to each other. At first, i.e., today, there will be criticisms articulated by high-ranking concerned scientists that there is too much lumping going on. Appropriately there will be finer and finer grids linking subethnic groups down to particular breeding populations, and no doubt a more sophisticated probability statistics to do this. There will be scholarly and popular arguments about where the boundaries are and who constitutes them. It follows that although categories such as "race" and "ethnic group" may well continue in popular usage, they will begin to acquire a meaning that is more particularizing and relational than whether the surname is Spanish. These categories will be redefined and will then feed back into the broader cultural classifications, with their political and social consequences, in ways well worth monitoring.

While the FBI constructs regional "arbitrary" VNTR computer networks, other workers will map other more directly functional systems. The Human Genome Mapping Library in New Haven is the world's largest computerized repository of human gene mapping information. With the progress of the Human Genome Initiative, whose efforts will provide a common series of maps, these various data will eventually merge. As one expert at the Cold Spring Harbor meeting put it, "With enough of these systems and variation in [noncoding VNTR] frequencies among populations, one could begin to look at it overall to infer racial origin." A colleague chimed in, "Even conventional genetic markers can occasionally give you precise racial data" (Westin 1989).

The last 30 years have been a period of historic cultural redefinition of the traditional categories in the West, from race to gender to age, emphasizing plasticity. To mention only a few examples: thousands of "older people" now run in marathons, genders have multiplied. This emphasis on plasticity is not disappearing, but it is being challenged and supplemented in a variety of cultural domains by the reintroduction of supposedly biological constraints and givens: for example, the PMS syndrome or gay gene. The power of the new genetics, biotechnology, and the Human Genome Initiative are providing "race" with a new legitimacy. However, the new techno-scientific understanding of population genetics will certainly be conflated with older cultural understandings of race, gender, and age. Some of the dangers inherent in this blurring are obvious; others are not. Once one has a database that meets all of Eric Lander's standards, should it be used to test to see if someone is "really" Hispanic before granting them an affirmative action slot? American history is replete with older models of racial proof which could be drawn on to justify such procedures. Of course, this trend is not restricted to the United States; groups in China are apparently demanding scientific proof of their (formerly culturally defined) minority status in order to be allowed to have more children.

The dangers of proceeding in the direction toward relegitimizing racial or ethnic biological categories in the forensic arena should be clear enough. However, simply opposing the use of biotechnologies in these arenas seems in equal parts futile and wrong. Perhaps we need to go back to Galton's regret. Perhaps some researchers should keep their data banks open for the possibility of looking for and discovering individual genetic variation. Perhaps the genes for fingerprints—so individualizing—would be the place to start looking. Surely the techno-scientific imagination at the end of the twentieth century is capable of finding thousands of distinctive alleles, ones not linked to race and temperament. Seek and ye shall find. Then Galton would continue to remain where he belongs—in purgatory.

REFERENCES

Ballantyne, J., G. Sensabaugh, and J. Witkowski, eds., 1989. *DNA Technology and Forensic Science.* Cold Spring Harbor, N.Y.: Cold Spring Harbor Laboratory Press.

Bertillon, Alphonse. *Une application pratique de l'anthropométrie.* Paris: N.p., 1881.

Bertillon, A., and Albert Chervin. *Anthropologie métrique, conseil pratique aux missionnaires, scientifiques, sur la manière de mesurer, de photographier, et de décrire des sujets vivants et des pièces anatomiques.* Paris: Imprimerie Nationale, 1909.

Fincher, J. 1989. "Lifting latents is now very much a high-tech matter." *Smithsonian* 20: 216.

Galton, Francis. 1892. *Finger Prints.* London: Macmillan.

Gianelli, P. 1980. "The admissibility of novel scientific evidence: Frye v. United States, a half-century later." *Columbia Law Review* 80: 1199.

Gould, S. J. 1981. *The Mismeasure of Man.* New York: Norton.

Harmon, R. P. 1989. "The Frye test: Considerations for DNA identification techniques." *Banbury Report* 32: 89.

Hicks, J. W. 1989. "FBI program for the forensic application of DNA technology." *Banbury Report* 32: 209.

Jeffreys, A. J., et al. "Applications of multilocus and single-locus minisatellite DNA probes in forensic medicine." *Banbury Report* 32: 283.

Kearney, J. 1990. "The combined DNA index system (CODIS): A theoretical model." In L. Kirby, ed., *DNA Fingerprinting: An Introduction,* p. 284.

Kirby, L., ed., 1990. *DNA Fingerprinting: An Introduction.* New York: Stockton Press.

Lander, E. 1989. "Population genetic considerations in the forensic use of DNA typing." *Banbury Report* 32: 143.

Neufeld, P. J. 1989. "Admissibility of new or novel scientific evidence in criminal cases." *Banbury Report* 32: 73.

Nye, R. 1984. *Crime, Madness and Politics in Modern France: The Medical Concept of National Decline.* Princeton: Princeton University Press.

Office of Technology Assessment (OTA). 1990. *Genetic Witness: Forensic Uses of DNA Tests.* Washington D.C.: U.S. Government Printing Office.

Putterman, M. 1990. "Probability and statistical analysis." In Kirby, *DNA Fingerprinting,* p. 176.

Rose, S., and T. Keith. 1989. "Standardization of systems: Essential or desirable?" *Banbury Report* 32: 319.

Wechsler, J. 1982. *A Human Comedy: Physiology and Caricature in Nineteenth Century Paris.* Chicago: University of Chicago Press.

Westin, A. F. 1989. "A privacy analysis of the use of DNA techniques as evidence in courtroom proceedings." *Banbury Report* 32: 25.

CHAPTER 7

Severing the Ties:
Fragmentation and Dignity
in Late Modernity

THE INTIMATE linkage between the two key symbolic arenas, "the body" and "the person," would have to figure prominently on any list of distinctively Western traits. Following the lead of the pioneering essays of Marcel Mauss on "Les Techniques du corps" (1950a) and "La Personne" (1950b), first anthropologists and then historians have documented the diversity of practices implicating "corporality" and "personhood." James Clifford, in his authoritative biography of Maurice Leenhardt, the French anthropologist and missionary who worked in New Caledonia and produced some of the most sensitive ethnographic analyses of the "person," writes: "Leenhardt never tired of recounting a conversation with Boesoou Erijisi in which he proposed to his oldest convert: 'In short, what we've brought into your thinking is the notion of spirit.' To which came the correction: 'Spirit? Bah! We've always known about the spirit. What you brought was the body' " (Clifford 1982; citing Leenhardt 1937). Leenhardt, the Protestant missionary pastor and ethnographer, shared with Marcel Mauss— the Jewish, socialist, and arm-chair anthropologist—a profound uneasiness about modernity. The price to be paid in human solidarity for the rise of the "individual" and "the body" was an important theme for both of these reluctant moderns, even if they both saw the rise of the individual as an evolutionary step that could not be reversed. Mauss wrote *The Gift* (1950c) to demonstrate how unique and late in world history the category of the "economic" really was and how much social and moral solidarity had been lost through its triumph. Leenhardt worried whether a person without concrete "participatory" supports was not condemned to be set adrift, alienated, and closed to communitas.

The case of *John Moore v. the Regents of the University of California* encapsulates many of the key elements in contemporary debates about the body, what its boundaries are, who owns it, and why these debates arouse our curiosity. John Moore sued the University of California after the doctors at U.C.L.A. Medical Center used matter removed from his body to produce an immortal cell line which they then patented. Moore claimed a share of the profits, arguing that the cells were his property. The California Supreme Court did not agree with Moore. While the law has spoken clearly in this case, the broader cultural issues of the body and the person, ethics, economics, and science remain very much open to debate and clarification.

A central argument of this essay is that it is not quite true, as is so often asserted, that it is the "newness" of contemporary technology that leaves us culturally unprepared. It is also the effacement of "oldness" of so many of the background assumptions and practices that lurk unexamined at the edges in these cases which contextualize the technology and frame our questions and responses. Identifying some of this background can help isolate elements of the unarticulated uneasiness that many feel over late modern culture. Put more starkly, having to choose between the long covered-over but still lingering residuum of Christian beliefs which hold "the body" to be a sacred vessel and the tenets of the market culture's "rational actor" view of the human person as contractual negotiator, choices unwittingly presented by several judges of the California Supreme Court in their opinions on the Moore case, can lead to melancholy or stress depending on your disposition. Today, both lines (the Christian and the liberal) are set within the framework of late capitalism, characterized in part by Frederic Jameson as the "prodigious expansion of capital into hitherto uncommodified areas," specifically nature (1991:36). My concern is with the cultural framing of that ongoing event.

The Moore case encapsulates another axis of change as well. Redrafting of the patent laws has crystallized and catalyzed changes in the practices and self-characterization of scientists, especially in the biosciences. Not only is the line between theoretical and practical science increasingly hard to draw, but the stakes and rewards are increasingly measured in terms of real capital in addition to the symbolic capital and authority the old system was based on. The morality tale told about the corruption of science by industry is belied, or at least made more complex, by the overwhelming involvement of the field's leaders in securing the bridgeheads. This development is a contingent culmination of older cultural processes, one step in an accelerated process in which truth and virtue were long ago separated. That epistemological separation, however, is only belatedly being given cultural form. Its acknowledgment, becoming harder and harder to resist, poses important problems about the authority of science in late modern society.

In sum, this essay is an attempt to map the regestalting of truth and virtue, body and person, through the examination of one case study. Following in the line of Max Weber and Michel Foucault, I want to chart the forms of life-regulation and the production of value emergent today among those we have authorized to speak the truth about life. This essay forms part of a larger project to analyze what Shapin and Schaffer, following Wittgenstein, have referred to as a form of life, linking material, discursive, and social technologies together. Whereas their object was the early modern social matrix in which the experimental life triumphed over Hobbes's Leviathan, mine is late modern society and culture in which the boundaries of the experimental life, and its older authority structures, are rapidly being withdrawn.[1]

NEW FORMS AND NEW NORMS OF TRUTH AND VIRTUE

In 1980 the Supreme Court of the United States ruled by a vote of 5–4 that new life forms fell under the jurisdiction of Federal patent law. General Electric microbiologist Ananda Chakrabarty had developed a novel bacterial strain capable of digesting oil slicks. Chakrabarty modified an existing bacterium by introducing DNA plasmids (circular strands of DNA carrying a specific gene) into the bacterial cells, thereby giving the organism the capacity to break down crude oil components. In so doing, he produced a new being with markedly different characteristics from any found in nature, one with the potential for significant utility. The Court ruling that Chakrabarty, having invented something "new" and "useful," found it appropriate to protect his invention with a patent.

A report from the U.S. Office of Technology Assessment underlined the dimension of the Court's decision that has drawn the most public attention: "The question of whether or not an invention embraces living matter is irrelevant to the issue of patentability, as long as the invention is the result of human intervention" (OTA 1987: 49). While it is true that previously (since 1930) plant forms had been patentable, a variety of factors—from the organization of the seed industry to the relatively limited ability to intervene efficiently and rapidly in plant varieties previous to the advent of genetic engineering—had contained the scope and impact of such patents until recently (see Kloppenburg 1990).

The Chakrabarty decision was less a legal milestone than an event which symbolized broader economic, political, and cultural changes taking place. The Supreme Court's ringing phrase that "Congress intended statutory subject matter to include anything under the sun that is made by man," coming as it did in the same year as the election of Ronald Reagan as President of the United States and as the massive influx of venture capital into the biotechnology world, can be appropriately picked as a signpost date for a new emergent constellation of knowledge and power. Although the encouragement of technology transfer, advances in genetic engineering, patent law precedents, and strong bipartisan pressure to reform patent law to protect American business all obviously had a longer (bipartisan) history, they arguably came together with new force in 1980.

In 1980, Congress passed the Patent and Trademark Amendment Act "to prompt efforts to develop a uniform patent policy that would encourage cooperative relationships between universities and industry, and ultimately take government-sponsored inventions off the shelf and into the marketplace" (OTA 1987: 7). At the time the government had some 25 different patent policies. This thicket of regulations tended to discourage exclusive licensing agreements which made industrial investment in product development less likely. The goal of the new policy was to encourage technological advance and a closer connections of university-based research with industry. Under the Act's provisions, universities were obliged to report any potentially patentable invention (Eisenberg 1987: 196). The universities responded with enthusiasm. An Office of Technology Assessment report on *New Developments in Biotechnology: Ownership of Human Tissues and Cells* reports that from 1980 to 1984 patent applications from universities in relevant human biological domains rose 300 percent. The creation of the Court of Appeals of the Federal Circuit, one of the Reagan administration's first acts, was a landmark event in its consolidation and systemization of patent cases. Patent law was being standardized and unified.

A threshold had been crossed; the 1980s witnessed a dramatic change in the institutional and normative relationships between American universities and the industrial world (see Dickinson 1984; Kenny 1986). A study by a Harvard team of the impact of these and related developments on the social organization of science and its normative structure showed that in 1986 industrial firms were supporting one-fourth of biotechnology research in institutions of higher education and that almost one-quarter of university scientists in departments relevant to biotechnology had industry support of some kind (see Blumenthal, Gluck, Louis, and Wise 1986; Blumenthal, Gluck, Louis, Stoto, and Wise 1986; Zuckerman 1988. 7). According to the report, scientists with ties to industry were five times as likely as their unindustrially connected colleagues to withhold research results from publication (Weil 1988). In a 1991 article titled "Academic-Corporate Ties in Biotechnology: A Quantitative Study," Sheldon Krimsky et al. extend the time-frame and scope of the Harvard study, documenting the acceleration of the trend toward increasing interconnection of the university-based biosciences with industry. Using a restricted definition of business ties (one requiring membership on a scientific advisory board, holding of a managerial position, substantial equity, or membership on the board of directors), the study indicates that in 1988, 37 percent of the biomedical scientists and geneticists who were members of the National Academy of Sciences had formal ties with the biotechnology industry. However, as membership in the academy is lifelong and as older members may have been less involved in the new scientific-corporate culture, Krimsky believes the percentage of active members with substantial industry ties may be as high as 50 percent (Krimsky et al. 1991: 275). The implication that the research elite of the biosciences in the United States have spearheaded the transition from separation between industry and the university to mutual dependency is confirmed by Krimsky's demonstration of the preponderant place of the most prestigious departments on advisory boards of biotechnology companies.

Krimsky offers two pertinent generalizations: "In less than a decade, the fields of molecular biology, genetics, and biochemistry in the United States have experienced a dual transformation. First, they have been transformed as basic sciences in the aftermath of the discoveries of gene splicing and gene synthesis. Second, they have been transformed as social institutions as the marriage between academic and industrial science was consummated" (Krimsky et al. 1991: 285). This marriage has altered both partners: the supposedly staid and pure university has entered head-over-heels into the commercial world: and the biotechnology wing of the industrial world, like the sectors of the computer industry before it, invented a modified industrial milieu incorporating elements of university life considered necessary to draw and keep top quality (often young) researchers. It is commonly agreed that, at least in the biosciences, the line between *basic* and *applied* research has been redrawn. Rebecca Eisenberg, a leading legal expert on patent laws, writes: "Not only has the historical time lag between the two collapsed, but it has become difficult to characterize given research problems as belonging in one category or the other. . . . [N]oteworthy scientific discoveries are made in industrial laboratories, and patentable inventions are made in university laboratories" (1987: 195–96). Sociologists and historians writing about these new institutional relationships tend to assume (no doubt correctly) that the general institutional norms of the biotechnology industry are basically like other businesses governed by profit, efficiency, and productivity. While attention has been focused on the impact of industry models on the academy, the reverse exchanges have been ignored. The biotechnology world (again like the computer industry before it) has its own particularities. Many companies have incorporated "libraries," "conferences," "publishing," "seminars," "visiting scholars," and the like to attract and keep talented and productive scientists. At least in the San Francisco Bay Area—with its high concentration of university scientists, biotech companies, and medical facilities—there is a good deal of movement across the university-industry boundary which has been facilitated by the academy becoming more industrial, while this sector of industry has mimicked elements of scholarly life in the biosciences. This mutual accommodation has many dimensions worth studying, not the least of which is the way it has facilitated the translation of academic status into industrial legitimacy in the world of venture capital, a world which has made industry possible in its current form. The most prestigious scientists are the most sought after and apparently the most open to being courted. New firms needing scientific legitimacy to raise venture capital are more likely to have prestigious scientific advisory boards, and these boards are most likely to be from the most prestigious universities. As Rebecca Eisenberg observes: "Capital markets are placing a dollar value on intellectual property long before a product is ready for market. The prospectus that high technology companies use to attract investment capital advertise the companies affiliations with university facilities and researchers" (1987: 196). Following Pierre Bourdieu, we can say that until recently producers of truth in the biosciences were rewarded mainly in symbolic capital, making them "dominated members of the dominating class" (1984). During the 1980's means were developed to turn symbolic capital into monetary capital and back again. Conversion of one form to the other has been facilitated and accelerated within this sector of the field of power and culture. An important element of more traditional bourgeois culture has been (late) modernized.

Krimsky et al. (1991) highlight three areas of controversy arising out of the new situation: conflicts of interest, shifts in research agenda, and potential obstacles of intellectual exchange. There is apparently some residual hesitancy about the new norms and

135

practices, as it is now not rare to find the scientific advisory boards membership classified as proprietary information. Others stipulate proprietary covenants with their advisers. The presence of industry-university ties in the biosciences is so pervasive that Krimsky et al. write that it "helps us to explain the emergence of a new climate in biology in which limited secrecy replaced free and open communication" (1991: 284). Anyone who has read James Watson's account (1968) of the race to discover the structure of the DNA molecule may well wonder how free and open the situation ever was. What has changed is the entry of money and patents. Watson and Crick were in mad pursuit of truth, prestige, and French *au pairs*. Today, if David Baltimore or Lee Hood were to write his autobiography, patents, exclusive licensing agreements, and consultant fees would be added to the narrative.

Peer review is central to the normative system of modern science. Objective and impartial judgment linked to an ethics of anonymity lies at the heart of the self-legitimization of modern science. Today, with so many peer reviewers having commercial ties, researchers submitting cutting-edge grant applications may well be leaving themselves open to losing a competitive advantage. Krimsky documents the large number of industry-connected peer reviewers involved in judging the scientific merit of governmental grants. He observes that it is not unlikely that scientists, themselves involved with industry and knowing that the only thing preventing their competitors (serving as peer reviewers) from appropriating their ideas is the code of ethics (which they themselves are actively engaged in rewriting), will decide that the risk of losing exclusivity is not worth the grant. This risk could well push prestigious and adventurous bioscientists to seek funds with industry directly.

The two universalized productions of Western bourgeois culture—technoscience and modern rationalized capitalism—have entered into a new relationship with each other. This merger has already yielded increased efficiency and production. However, its very success recasts the question of authority for scientists. Having made a new Faustian contract, members of the bioscience community are culturally ill-equipped to reflect on their own

136

practices given their generalized abandonment of *bildung* (for all the keening about political correctness taking place today, it is often forgotten that the major curricular reforms were brought about by the elimination of general education requirements often at the behest of scientists with no time to waste), and they must now face the consequences of their own acts, their voluntary and willful self-formation. Particularly within the biosciences, the undermining of their own legitimacy and authority is largely an autoproduction. The best and the brightest in this self-labeled meritocratic community have led the way. Symbolic, monetary, and political capital are now in a tight feedback loop. Judged by the older "Mertonian" norms, which many in the bioscience community still include in their self-conception and in their authorizing practices, they are in a weak rhetorical position to weep over their lost honor.

Disinterestedness needs a new vocabulary. More than even before, the legitimacy of the biosciences now rests on claims to produce health. Having tilted too heavily in the direction of quasi-utilitarian ends ("quasi" is that "health," like wealth, is a symbolic medium subject to inflation and deflation), the bioscience community now runs the risk that merely producing truth will be insufficient to move the venture capitalists, patent offices, and science writers on whom the biosciences are increasingly dependent for their new-found wealth. In the case we are leading up to, *John Moore v. the Regents of the University of California*, the normative element that irked the Supreme Court judges the most was "disinterestedness," even if avarice and ambition were peripheral to the central legal issues of the case. What is troubling to informed common sense is the existence of a gap between the purported character of the truth-seeker and the scientific results.

Michel Foucault saw the severing of the "ethical subject" from the "truth-seeking subject" as an important element in modernity and a distinctive characteristic of Western culture. He observed that until the seventeenth century, it was widely, perhaps universally, held that to know the truth one had to be virtuous, that is, capable and worthy of knowing. Descartes's philosophy constitutes a cultural break of major proportions. Descartes's views

137

amounted to saying: "To accede to truth, it suffices that I be *any* subject which can see what is evident. . . . Thus, I can be immoral and know the truth. I believe that this is an idea which, more or less explicitly, was rejected by all previous cultures. Before Descartes, one could not be impure, immoral, and know the truth. With Descartes, direct evidence is enough. After Descartes, we have a nonascetic subject of knowledge. This change makes possible the institutionalization of modern sciences" (Foucault 1984: 371–72). Foucault points out that Western thought was uneasy about this break, and many thinkers sought to reestablish a relationship between truth-seeking and moral norms. At the very least, after 1980 we are confronted with a new historical turning in the long story of the relations of truth and virtue, power and culture. One thing is equally clear: piety, moralism, or nostalgia will not set things straight.

Mo Better Cell Line

On July 9, 1990, the Supreme Court of the State of California handed down its decision in the case of John Moore v. the Regents of the University of California et al. A divided Court ruled that Mr. Moore did *not* have the *property* rights in cells taken from his body, transformed into an immortalized cell line and patented by a team at the U.C.L.A. Medical Center. At the same time, the Court unanimously agreed that John Moore did have the right to a trial for damages on betrayal of the fiduciary relationship. There are a number of different lines—legal, ethical, technoscientific, medical, textual, economic, and media(ic)—which converge in this case. The legal issues are multiple, beginning with tort law, including fiduciary issues, and extending to property law. The scientific dimensions of the case seem to have received little attention either in the court proceedings or in the media coverage.[2]

According to the allegations of John Moore's complaint, assumed as true by the California Supreme Court for purposes of its decision, the essential facts are as follows. John Moore, a surveyor by trade working in Alaska, was diagnosed as suffering from a rare disease, hairy cell leukemia. Moore sought further medical advice from one of the three internationally recognized specialists on the disease, David W. Golde, a professor of medicine at U.C.L.A. and then head of the Department of Hematology-Oncology. Moore became a patient at the U.C.L.A. Medical Center in August 1976, where the diagnosis was confirmed. Dr. Golde advised Moore to have his spleen removed, a surgically routine procedure, as this seemed to prolong life-expectancy, albeit for medically poorly understood reasons. Moore agreed, signing a standard consent form to the operation on or about October 19, 1976. His spleen was successfully removed. His condition then "stabilized"; that is, although Moore was not cured of cancer, its progression was halted for an unknown period of time. Cancer cells are still present in his blood, but the cells are neither proliferating nor destabilizing the body.

Subsequent to the operations, Moore returned to the U.C.L.A. Medical Center periodically between November 1976 and September 1983 (approximately ten times) at the request of Dr. Golde. On each visit Golde ordered samples of blood or blood serum, and on at least one occasion skin, bone marrow aspirate, and sperm samples, telling Moore that his bodily products had certain "unique characteristics," with potential research interest as well as implications for "the betterment of humanity."[3] At least one of the trips was paid for by U.C.L.A. from Golde's grant money. During one of his visits in 1983, Moore was given a new consent form to sign granting the university rights to his cell line and bodily products. This new form was required by University regulations because Golde wanted to draw blood not only for therapeutic purposes but also for scientific research purposes as well. Moore, his suspicions aroused by what he considered to be evasive answers as to the purpose of these examinations on the part of Dr. Golde, refused to sign the form. After renewed requests by Dr. Golde for him to sign the consent form, Moore contacted an attorney (Cranor 1989: 200).

The minimal elements necessary for an understanding of the case are the following. Shortly before Moore's splenectomy, the defendant, David Golde, instructed his research associate, Shirley Quan, to obtain a specimen of the surgically removed spleen "to study and characterize the nature of its cells and substance before its destruction" (CT). Golde and Quan immortalized the cells taken from Moore's spleen into a new cell line they called "Mo cell line," before August 1979. This means they succeeded in making the cells reproduce themselves indefinitely rather that dying off after a finite number of divisions, not always an easy thing to achieve. Immortalizing a cell line makes it available as a research tool. Golde was aware that certain of Moore's blood products were of potentially great value and would provide "competitive, commercial, and scientific advantages" (CT). None of these research procedures were directly related to Moore's medical care. Moore was informed in general terms of what Golde and his team were doing and, following the law, his permission was explicitly requested. In August 1979, Golde took the first step toward applying for a patent. The patent covers by-products of the Mo cell line to produce certain proteins. The patent was applied for in 1979, amended in 1983, and eventually granted to the Regents of the University of California on March 20, 1984.[4] Dr. Golde became a paid consultant of Genetics Institute, acquiring 75,000 shares of common stock at a nominal price. Genetics Institute paid a pro-rata share of Golde's salary and fringe benefits in exchange for exclusive access to the materials and research performed. The large multinational pharmaceutical company Sandoz joined the agreement in 1982, increasing Golde's and the Regents reimbursement. As we described earlier, such arrangements were becoming standard parts of the institutional and cultural landscape of the biosciences in the 1980s.

John Moore, his leukemia stabilized, alleged no medical malpractice or physical injury. Rather, he held that having been monitored for more than therapeutic reasons, he should have been informed of Golde's specific research and financial interests. Moore also claimed a "conversion" interest, i.e., that his property (his cells and blood products) was illegally converted for someone else's profit. Media coverage has frequently blurred the two issues: (1) breach of Golde's fiduciary trust and/or lack of informed consent; (2) conversion of property. This blurring has added to a confused public reception of the case and its implications. The California Supreme Court ruled that although John Moore had no conversion, i.e., property rights, there was "a cause or action for breach of the physician's disclosure obligations" (CT). Under California law, a physician is obliged to "disclose personal interests unrelated to the patient's health, whether research or economic, that may affect his medical judgment" (CT). The Court held that Golde could be sued either for breach of fiduciary trust or for not obtaining Moore's informed consent. Golde argued that he had informed Moore that he had a research interest in his case but was under no legal obligation to do more than this. As one of the Supreme Court justices argued, while it seemed obvious to common sense that Moore had not been treated fairly and openly, it was nonetheless better not "to force the round pegs of privacy and dignity into the square hole of property in order to protect the patient, since the fiduciary and informed consent theories protect these interests directly by requiring full disclosure" (CT). The case is now pending trial on breach of fiduciary duty to obtain informed consent.

State Supreme Court Decision

Two lower court decisions preceded the State Supreme Court decision. In the first, the Superior Court upheld the University by holding that Moore's limited informed consent to the medical procedures at a university research hospital was unqualified. In other words, John Moore had entered a research hospital, had his medical condition appropriately treated, and by signing a standard consent form for splenectomy had released the doctors to do research on the detached body parts and substances. At the second level, a divided Court of Appeals reversed the Superior Court decision. The Court's majority opinion held that surgically removed human tissue was the patient's "tangible private property" (CT). It followed that without Moore's explicit permission the University's use of the tissue constituted a conversion. The minority dissent argued against the application of private property principles to surgical tissue, absent legislative enactment. The theme that this was new legal terrain for which legislative guidance was required was echoed at the Supreme Court. It was implied by at least two court decisions that some wrong was done in the case,

141

but they differ as to where to locate it. The judges on several occasions and at several levels of the court system suggest that, as with legislation covering the transplant of organs, it would be appropriate for the state legislature to develop a regulatory policy. They held that it was not the function of the courts to make law, only to interpret existing law.

The core issues presented to the California Supreme Court were: (1) Does the unqualified consent to medical surgery at a teaching and research hospital permit the scientific study of the removed tissue? (2) Should the Court extend the definition of personal property and the law of conversion to make tortuous a post-surgery scientific study of tissues removed with patient consent? The Regents' attorneys argued on (1) that anyone entering a University research hospital for treatment was tacitly seeking the benefit of the hospital's research which preceded their admission. It followed that there was implicit consent to the very procedures from which they sought to benefit, that is, ongoing scientific research. Moore in fact had admitted, in an amended complaint, that he was aware of the scientific interest of his condition, implying a presumption of consent. Finally, his silence for eight years after the operation further strengthened the presumption of consent.

The Regents argued on (2) that although the law does recognize a variety of interests in one's own body, it has never created a property right in surgically removed body parts. The closest legal precedent is found in the next-of-kin's interest in the body of the deceased. The family has the right to dispose of the corpse but not to sell it. This is a quasi-property right based on the common law refusal to recognize any property rights in corpses. Common law interpreted the matter as a religious one, traditionally leaving it to the domain of ecclesiastical courts. No longer having ecclesiastical courts, American state courts invented the notion of quasi-property as a means of allowing next-of-kin to dispose of the body (but not to sell it or transfer the right). The Regents' attorney extended this analogy to therapeutically removed tissue. Sentiment, they say, is involved but not property rights. Further, since therapeutic tissue and dead bodies no longer support an individual's existence, the law regarding their dominion and disposition addresses the similar public policy of community health and safety without concern for personal injury or breach of personal liberty. Hence, there is no right for patient ownership of tissue therapeutically removed by surgical procedure. As there is no property right, the body cannot be the subject of conversion.

The modern precedents for the lack of conversion are found in hospitals claim to remove corneas from deceased persons for transplant purposes without express consent. Courts in various states including California have held that individual rights of property, liberty, or privacy were secondary to public health considerations in such matters. The ensuing blindness of those who would be refused the transplant are set in balance against individual rights, and consequently the state has a public health obligation to make the corneas available. Legal scientific access to tissue is recognized and regulated in a number of ways. In California there are four means to access lawfully tissue for scientific study. The Uniform Anatomical Gift Act provides for gifts to advance medical science. The unclaimed Dead Body Statute provides access to human tissue for scientific study. Legal access is provided by the removal of pathologic or diagnostic tissue in medical treatment (subject to informed consent) and the removal of tissue for expressed research purposes. These precedents amount to a strong public presumption against private property claims to tissue or body parts. These regulations provide for the use of tissue or transfer of organs as a gift. Through these regulatory mechanisms, public health, safety, and scientific advance are set in balance with liberty and personal tort interests.

Moore Decision: No Conversion

The majority decision held: "To establish conversion, plaintiff must establish an actual interference with his *ownership* or *right of possession*. . . . Where plaintiff neither has title to the property alleged to have been converted, nor possession thereof, he cannot maintain an action of conversion" (CT). California statutes for organs, blood, fetuses, pituitary glands, corneal tissues, and dead bodies deal with human biological materials as objects *res nulles*, regulating their disposition to achieve policy goals. The court held that there is no precedent for conversion liability for the use

143

of human cells in medical research. The extension of conversion law into this area will hinder research by restricting access to the necessary raw materials. To do so would be to impose on scientists a tort duty to investigate the consensual pedigree for each human cell sample used in research. Further, it might grant Moore ownership of the genetic code for lympokines which had the same biochemical makeup in all humans. The Court expressed a reluctance to extend the tort law into this domain, suggesting that if such an extension were to be made it was the legislature that would most properly do so.

DIGNITY AND IMMORTALITY IN LATE MODERNITY

In a concurring opinion, Justice Arabian, a conservative, expressed his sense of outrage that something fundamentally morally wrong had taken place. However, he argued that affirming Moore's property claims would only compound that moral wrong: "Plaintiff has asked us to recognize and enforce a right to sell one's own body tissue for profit. He entreats us to regard the human vessel—the single most venerated and protected subject in any civilized society—as equal with the basest commercial commodity. He urges us to commingle the sacred with the profane. He asks much" (CT). Jurgen Habermas labels "neoconservatives" those who embrace technical and economic change while refusing cultural change. The label fits the judge. Justice Arabian writes of a venerated vessel which he equates with the civilized subject. He asks much. However, acknowledging that links between the sacred and the profane must be forged in a capitalist society, Justice Arabian proposes a remedy for this sacrilege that is somewhat modern: the public good would be best protected in a legislated profit-sharing system between donor and researcher. While such a scheme might well produce a form of equity, it is not clear how it protects the sanctity of the vessel.

In a fifty-page dissent the liberal Justice Mosk expresses general moral dismay. He first retells the story of the undermining of supposedly traditional norms of science and medicine through the

144

seduction of commercial motives. The Justice's outrage turns primarily on the Mertonian norm of disinterestedness. Drawing a distinction between a "truly scientific use" and a "blatant commercial exploitation," he argues that while it is fortuitous if the results of pure science happen to find a commercial application, however, if scientific activity seeks such gain from the outset, such motivation constitutes a betrayal. He concludes: "If this science has become science for profit, then we fail to see any justification for excluding the patient from participation in those profits" (CT). Secrecy and greed are not genuine scientific motives and pollute the truth-seeker. Once motivation is sullied by dreams of commerce, then everyone has an equal right to lucre as well. Fair is fair.

Justice Mosk is equally incensed by a further transgression, this time not only of scientific ethics but of what he identifies as the culture's most central values: "Our society acknowledges a profound ethical imperative to respect the human body as the physical and temporal expression of the unique human persona" (CT). Such research tends to treat the body as a commodity—a means to a profitable end. This commodification violates "the dignity and sanctity with which we regard the human whole, body as well as mind and soul" (CT). Perhaps the judge employed the couplet "dignity and sanctity" as a trope to underline the seriousness of the matter. However, having just defended a secular market view of patient and doctor as a counterbalance to what he considered as unilateral corruption, albeit with a certain uneasiness, his evocation of sanctity seems curious. In any case, the central equation remains a holistic one: body, mind, spirit, and person are one; part is whole.

"Dignity," although a seemingly innocuous term to employ, is, in fact, strikingly heuristic. Ernest Kantorowicz, in his *The King's Two Bodies: A Study in Medieval Political Theology*, provides a detailed discussion of the origin of the term and its role in Western law and politics. *Dignitas* derived from the myth of the Phoenix. According to the ancient Greek myth, there was only one Phoenix alive at any one time. After some five hundred years, the bird set his nest ablaze, fanned the fire with the wings, and perished in the flames,

145

while from the glowing cinders a new bird arose. The new Phoenix, the same and different as the one that perished, provided a central symbol of resurrection. Philosophically, the whole kind is preserved in the individual. The species and the individual coincided: the species immortal and the individual mortal. The Phoenix was at once individual and collective because the whole species produced no more than a single specimen at a time. *Dignitas* was at first an attribute to the King: The King is dead, long live the King. Then the term migrated to the medieval corporation. *Dignitas* became generalized and was given a precise legal status as a Phoenix-like attribute in which the corporation coincided with the individual precisely because it reproduced no more than one individuation at a time, the incumbent—the corporate soul.

In this sense, Moore's body was inviolable and unique, even in its immortalized state, simultaneously the same and different. In fact, Mosk seems to hold precisely this view when he asserts that Moore's cells and his cell line are identical even though the cell line has a different number of chromosomes and exists only under laboratory conditions. Justice Mosk might well agree with Damasus, a Canonist, who wrote in 1215: *"Dignitas nunquam perit"* (the dignity never perishes, although individuals die every day; Kantorowicz 1957: 385). Evoking this snippet of genealogy is intended to highlight the endurance of long-standing cultural formulations which still seem to have signifying potential. Contemporary technical capacities, however, now raise a range of possibilities for new practices and hence new meaning which overflow the older vessels. In this context, it is the vessels and their attributes which warrant re-examination.

RESURRECTED BODIES

The long tradition of belief in the resurrection of the body in Christian doctrine and practices is especially striking. Caroline Walker Bynum provides us with a rich discussion of these issues in her book, *Fragmentation and Redemption: Essays on Gender and the Human Body in Medieval Religion*. She writes, "Christian preachers and theologians from Tertullian to the seventeenth-century divines asserted that God will assemble the decayed and fragmented corpses of human beings at the end of time and grant them eternal life and incorruptibility" (1991: 239). This central tenet of educated Christian belief and practice for over a millennia and a half (and of popular belief for another half millennia) was meant *literally*. Learned debates raged over what would happen to fingernails discarded over the course of a lifetime on the day of judgment. Which ones would the resurrected body have? Great thinkers, sure to figure on the list of Great Books, such as saints Augustine and Aquinas, took the question of resurrection of the body in its literal materiality quite seriously. Furthermore, the attention given to such issues, while seemingly arcane, cannot be dismissed as "scholastic," because concern with resurrection was widespread and hardly restricted to an elite.

The resurrection of the body was an established element of Christian faith between the second and fifth centuries. Debates raged over details precisely because of the consensus. By 1215, the Fourth Lateran Council required assent to the proposition that all will rise again in their individual bodies. The *Libri Quatuor Sententiarum* of Peter of Lombard, the twelfth-century theologian and Bishop of Paris, set the terms of the debate on doctrinal issues for the following several centuries. Peter of Lombard's *Sentences* is a compilation of opinions and doctrines whose open-endedness and lack of originality was apparently one of the central reasons for its enduring importance. Richard McKeon writes of the *Sentences*: "From the thirteenth to the sixteenth century perhaps no single book exercised an influence in education and in the development of philosophical and theological sciences comparable" to it (1929: 185). Peter posed questions such as the following: "What age, height, and sex will we have in the resurrected body? Will all matter that has passed through the body at any point be resurrected? Must bits of matter return to the particular members (fingernails or hair, for example) where they once resided?" (McKeon 1929: 242). The question of cannibalism and the resurrection, debated since the second century, achieved a kind of renaissance in the thirteenth: if humans ate other humans, in which person would the common matter arise? It was decided that digested food did become part of "the substance of human nature" and would rise at the end of time. Thomas Aquinas reflected upon a more complicated case: what of the fate of a man who ate *only* human embryos, who in turn generated a child who ate only human embryos? Since human matter will arise only in the one who possessed it first, this child will not rise at all. Echoing the title of her book, *Fragmentation and Redemption*, Bynum writes, "Scholastic theologians worried not about whether the body was crucial to human nature but about how part related to whole—that is, how bits could and would be reintegrated after scattering and decay" (1991: 253). Bynum argues that it is the exoticism, the seeming nonsensicalness of the beliefs, practices, and debates over the body's resurrection, which is, upon closer inspection, precisely what needs to be taken seriously in order to understand better these Christians and, consequently, ourselves. For contemporary, educated moderns it is the literalness, the sheer materialism of what is now taken to be the spiritualist Middle Ages, that makes the doctrine of resurrection seem so exotic.

A turning point in the theological debate took place with Thomas Aquinas's rearticulation of Aristotle's definition of the soul as the form of the body. This "hylomorphic" view (that is, the union of the soul and the body as form to matter) achieved a dramatic reduction of the identity claims of matter. If the soul is the form of our body, then all matter must be "so to speak, packed into the soul" (Bynum 1991: 255). Aquinas's theory of form solved many problems, for example, individual fingernails were not the person, only soul-formed matter constituted substance and would be resurrected. The attachment of the body/person metonymy—like questions of part and whole, fragmentation and redemption—was so pervasive that, whatever its logical appeal, Thomas's position took centuries to obtain full authority even among theologians. Among the faithful, hylomorphism was resisted or simply ignored for an even longer time. The great popularity of the relic cults in the thirteenth century practically imposed on the theologians a respect for the body, however fragmented, as the enduring locus of redemption. A belief in a fundamental identity between the body and the person was embedded in these popular beliefs and practices and was not to be shaken by theological finesse. Peter the Venerable wrote: "I have confidence more certainly than in any human thing that you ought not to feel contempt for the bones of the present martyrs as if they were dry bones but should honor them now full of life as if they were in their future incorruption . . . Flesh flowers from dryness and youth is remade from old age" (Bynum 1991: 265).

Christianity in its elevated reflections and in the practices of the pious maintained an uneasy tension between the wholeness of the body, its parts, the person, and fate, whose fascinating complexities deserve further attention. Certainly, one of the West's particularities is to be found in the tension between the body, as a mere thing carried by a triumphant science and technology, and the still present sense that the body and its parts are always more than things.

Bynum shows that modern philosophic attempts to strip these medieval discussions of their apparent absurdity by refusing to entertain them seriously founder on the enduring cultural understanding that the "person" is inextricably tied to the sheer materiality of the body of its parts (the brain being the contemporary candidate). Bynum demonstrates that analytic philosophers seem to find it "impossible to envision personal survival without material continuity" (Bynum 1991: 247). Bynum quotes research on organ transplants in America which reveals a common belief that more than organized matter is transplanted; some shred of identity is passed on to the recipient as well.

Today, for others, however, it is less "the body" than fragmented body matter which has potential value to industry, science, and the individual. The approach to "the body" found in contemporary biotechnology and genetics fragments it into a potentially discrete, knowable, and exploitable reservoir of molecular and biochemical products and events. By reason of its commitment to fragmentation, there is literally no conception of the person as a whole underlying these particular technological practices. In and of itself, this shift away from an organismic focus is neither good nor bad. However, it does seem to be confusing and troubling, especially when efforts are made to fit it into other value spheres, where different narratives of responsibility and personhood are found. Of course, we must hasten to add that these narratives are themselves in a process of fragmentation and change as well.

A transformed piece of matter from John Moore now lives forever, reduplicating itself over and over again in jars slowly rotating on racks in a temperature-controlled room in Maryland. The cell line is available upon the completion of a form from the requisite institutions and the payment of a nominal fee for handling. These immortalized bits and pieces can then be used to pursue more knowledge, to produce more health, to yield more profit. Anthropologically, it is this characteristically late modern environment which arouses our curiosity and concern.

Acknowledgments

Gratitude for their help are due, and warmly offered, to David Hess, Michael Meranze, Tom White, and especially Allen B. Wagner. The claims of the paper and its faults are my own.

Notes

1. See Weber (1946) and Shapin and Schaffer (1985).
2. I intend to deal with these in another paper.
3. *Ed. note:* Unless otherwise indicated, citations in this paragraph and the following pages are from the Court Transcript, indicated with a "CT" following the citation.
4. The scientific element of this history has been largely ignored by the Court as well as in the scholarly and mass media coverage. I treat it in another essay.

References

Blumenthal, D., M. Gluck, K. Louis, and D. Wise. 1986. "Industrial Support of University Research in Biotechnology." *Science* 231 (January 17): 242–46.

Blumenthal, D., M. Gluck, K. Louis, M. Soto, and D. Wise. 1986. "University-Industry Research Relationships in Biotechnology: Implications for the University." *Science* 232 (June 13): 1361–66.

Bourdieu, P. 1984. *Distinction*. Cambridge, Mass.: Harvard University Press.

Bynum, C. W. 1991. "Material Continuity, Personal Survival, and the Resurrection of the Body: A Scholastic Discussion in Its Medieval and Modern Contexts." In *Fragmentation and Redemption: Essays on Gender and the Human Body in Medieval Religion*, pp. 239–97. New York: Zone Books.

Clifford, J. 1982. *Person and Myth: Maurice Leenhardt in the Melanesian World*. Berkeley: University of California Press.

Cranor, C. F. 1989. "Patenting Body Parts: A Sketch of Some Moral Issues." In *Owning Scientific and Technical Information: Value and Ethical Issues*, ed. Vivian Weil and John W. Snapper, pp. 200–12. New Brunswick, N.J.: Rutgers University Press.

Dickinson, D. 1984. *The New Politics of Science*. New York: Pantheon Books.

Eisenberg, R. S. 1987. "Proprietary Rights and the Norms of Science in Biotechnology Research." *Yale Law Journal* 97 (2): 186–97.

Foucault, M. 1984. "On the Genealogy of Ethics: An Overview of Work in Progress." Interview with Paul Rabinow and Hubert Dreyfus in *The Foucault Reader*, ed. Paul Rabinow, pp. 340–72. New York: Pantheon Books.

Jameson, F. 1991. "The Cultural Logic of Late Capitalism." In *Postmodernism or, The Cultural Logic of Late Capitalism*, pp. 1–54. Durham, N.C.: Duke University Press.

Kantorowicz, E. H. 1957. *The King's Two Bodies: A Study in Medieval Political Theology*. Princeton, N.J.: Princeton University Press.

Kenny, M. 1986. *Biotechnology: The University-Industrial Complex*. New Haven: Yale University Press.

Kloppenburg Jr., J. 1990. *First the Seed: The Political Economy of Plant Biotechnology, 1492–2000*. Cambridge, U.K.: Cambridge University Press.

Krimsky, S., J. Ennis, and R. Weissman. 1991. "Academic-Corporate Ties in Biotechnology: A Quantitative Study." *Science, Technology, and Human Values* 16 (3): 275–87.

Leenhardt, M. 1937. *Do Kamo: La personne et le mythe dans le monde mélanésien*. Paris: Gallimard. (Trans. Basia Gulatis as *Do Kamo: Person and Myth in the Melanesian World*. Chicago: University of Chicago Press, 1979).

McKeon, R., ed. 1929. *Selections from Medieval Philosophers*. New York: Scribner's.

Mauss, M. 1950a. "Une Categorie de l esprit humaine: La notion de personne, cell de moi." In *Sociologie et Anthropologie*, ed. Claude Lévi-Strauss, Paris: Presses Universitaires de France (orig. 1934). (Trans. Ben Brewster as "A Category of the Human Mind," in *Sociology and Psychology*, pp. 57–95. London: Routledge and Kegan Paul, 1979.)

———. 1950b. "Les Techniques du corps." (Trans. Ben Brewster as "Body Techniques," in *Sociology and Psychology*, pp. 95–123. London: Routledge and Kegan Paul, 1979.)

151

————. 1950c. " Essai sur le don." In *Sociologie et Anthropologie*, ed. Claude Lévi-Strauss. Paris: Presses Universitaires de France (orig. 1938). (Trans. Ian Cunnison as *The Gift*. New York: Norton, 1967.)

Office of Technology Assessment (OTA). 1987. *New Developments in Biotechnology: Ownership of Human Tissues and Cells.* Washington, D.C.: Government Printing Office.

Shapin, S., and S. Schaffer. 1985. *Leviathan and the Air-Pump.* Princeton, N.J.: Princeton University Press.

Watson, J. 1968. *The Double Helix: A Personal Account of the Discovery of the Structure of DNA.* New York: Atheneum.

Weber, M. 1946. "Religious Rejections of the World and Their Directions." In *From Max Weber,* ed. Hans Gerth and C. Wright Mills, pp. 323–69. New York: Oxford University Press.

Weil, V. 1988. "Policy Incentives and Constraints." *Science, Technology, and Human Values* 13 (1 & 2): 17–26.

Zuckerman, H. 1988. "Introduction: Intellectual Property and Diverse Rights of Ownership in Science." *Science, Technology, and Human Values* 13 (1 & 2): 7–16.

CHAPTER 8

Steps Toward a Third Culture

> While orienting myself in order to frame what I
> expected to be fieldwork on the Human Genome
> Project I found several older texts to be helpful.
> Although a variety of events produced a swerve
> away from direct ethnographic engagement with
> the American genome project, the questions
> and problematizations provided by C. P. Snow,
> Hans Blumenberg, and Friedrich Nietzsche
> remained more than pertinent.[1]

TWO CULTURES

C. P. Snow's 1959 Rede Lectures at Cambridge identified and
lamented a divide between Science, i.e. physics, and the Traditional Culture, i.e., literature. Snow's pamphlet opened a passion-
ate debate about the existence and significance of this en-
trenched cultural separation. Following Bronislaw Malinowski,
Snow observed that scientists have a culture not only in the intel
lectual but in the anthropological sense: "without thinking about
it, they respond alike. That is what a culture means."[2] Simple! An
ethos informs that culture: pragmatic optimism. Scientists are
"impatient to see if something can be done: and inclined to think
it can be done, unless it's proved otherwise."[3] Snow captures the
physicists' stance toward themselves and the world with one of
those aphorisms that draw immediate assent but whose ironies
and ambiguities linger hauntingly. Snow remarked that these
men of science "naturally had the future in their bones."[4] Confident to the point of arrogance, pragmatic, often on the left of the
political spectrum, carriers of the future, if not in their bones at
least in their labs, these men of science surprised Snow, however,
by their lack of traditional culture, capital C, capital T. "The ear,

to some extent, the eye. Of books, though, very little. They are self-impoverished."[5]

The bearers of Traditional Literary Culture—the other Culture—were equally, if inversely, impoverished by their lack of scientific education. While this state of affairs, this relationship, remains more or less the same today, one important element of the situation has changed. Snow's observation that "it is the traditional culture, to an extent remarkably little diminished by the scientific one, which manages the western world," today sounds truly exotic, a report from a distant world. Those who currently manage us are imbued with neither of the two cultures although they certainly pay obeisance to techno-science in either its military or medical guise. In the intervening years, Snow's Oxbridge class culture was "modernized" under the Thatcher regime and its traces were eliminated in the U.S. ruling circles decades ago.

In his "Second Look," written several years later in response to the storm of reaction his book occasioned, Snow introduced several modifications to his position. First, he displaced physics from its throne, awarding molecular biology the right to represent the kingdom of science precisely because of its potential social impact. Molecular biology, he thought, "is likely to affect the way in which men think of themselves more profoundly than any scientific advance since Darwin's—and probably more so than Darwin's."[6] Second, he downplayed the significance of the distinction between science and technology, observing that in practice they were increasingly the same thing. He cites the work on the hemoglobin molecule as a fundamental scientific contribution whose discovery was inextricably linked to technology and health. Finally, Snow acknowledged that a Third Culture was emerging, social history, which would apply empirical methods to the cherished beliefs and assumptions held by members of the Literary Culture. It would presumably do something similar for the sciences.

Snow closes his Second Look with an observation and a question whose juxtaposition is quite striking. The observation: "We know that the vast majority, perhaps two-thirds, of our fellow men are living in the immediate presence of illness and premature death; their expectation of life is half of ours, most are under-nourished, many are near to starving, many starve . . . this suffering is unnecessary and can be lifted. If we don't know it, there is no excuse or absolution for us." The question: "How far is it possible to share the hopes of the scientific revolution, the modest difficult hopes for other human lives, and at the same time participate without qualification in [modernist] literature?"[7] If we substitute cultivated and critical thought at a world scale for literature, we still can and must ask ourselves this question.

Snow's challenge, his insistence on a new *bildung*, takes on a specific pertinence for us today, in part, because of what Snow indicated, the advances of molecular biology. More specifically yet, the Human Genome Initiative has allocated three percent of its budget to studying the social, ethical, and legal implications of its enterprise. If this gesture, whatever its motivations, is to take on any real meaning, then some hard work lies ahead. Hard work on ourselves. Hard work, to be sure, for practitioners of the human sciences, learning the fundamentals of molecular biology and genetics. Attaining a basic literacy in molecular biology and genetics is not that difficult in large part because of the lack of mathematics in the field. Furthermore, the work is highly rewarding.

A more difficult challenge lies on the other side of the divide: there is not much evidence of a reciprocating will to work on the self. Merely allocating money to support a growing community of professional ethicists and then parroting a few commonplaces about "hard choices" will not do. It won't do for two reasons. First, it is certain to produce more procedural specialists and more moralism; whatever else America lacks, it is not therapists and managers of the soul. Second, such a division of labor won't change the habits and practices of the scientists. The best among them perhaps will pledge three percent of their time to posing dilemmas and then get on with their scientific work exactly as before. That is to say, in a very precise manner—it won't have any ethical impact on them. One might well wonder what, if anything, is wrong with that? One way to approach that question is to ask how is it that scientists are not more theoretically curious about such matters?

155

THEORETICAL CURIOSITY

Hans Blumenberg's magisterial *The Legitimacy of the Modern Age* provides one of the most sweeping cultural and philosophical interpretations of Western rationality since Max Weber. Its historical perspective, especially Blumenberg's reflections on "The Trial of Theoretical Curiosity," can, I believe, help us situate and reflect on our current self-understanding, our common diverse responses, our cultures.[8] Blumenberg underlines that in the Ancient world the task of theory "was not to make life possible but to make it happy." [9] There was an order to the cosmos and philosophy's task was to understand that order and live in accordance with it. In the Christian Middle Ages, curiosity was still linked to and limited by virtue, but the telos was salvation, not happiness.

It was this new telos which led to what Blumenberg calls the trial of theoretical curiosity. Although there are roots of suscipion about curiosity among the Epicurians and the Stoics, it was the Catholic Church that turned this caution into a judicial and coercive affair. The problem was that theoretical curiosity has always refused to be limited either by 'humility' or 'child-like faith.' Hence, theoretical curiosity (Augustine identifies it as one of his worst and most intractable dispositions to sin) is specifically anti-church. Blumenberg argues that the reaction to the church's persecution of free inquiry opened the philosophic path to modernity—a second more subtle, and as yet unresolved, trial of theoretical curiosity.[10]

Maupertuis

Blumenberg nominates the philosopher Pierre Louis Moreau de Maupertuis (1698–1759) as emblematic of Enlightenment curiosity and as a precursor of modern times. This "functionary and hero of curiosity" combined a capacity to imagine scientific projects and an insistent political appeal to the powerful people of his time to support them. Maupertuis proposed a series of research projects which required collective and international cooperation, crossing territorial units and thus necessitating a certain political substructure to accomplish them. In his *Letter on the Progress of the Sciences*, he draws a distinction between those sciences which subsist and prosper on their own and those which require the power of Sovereigns for their fruition. The latter are those which require expenses beyond the means of any private individual or those experiments which "in the ordinary state of affairs [*l'ordre ordinaire*] could not be done."[11] Maupertuis proposes a global voyage to chart new lands hoping to find spices as well as creatures reportedly half-man, half-ape. He proposes mines, astronomical observatories, a grouping of the scientific insights of all nations, a universal city in which all scholars would speak Latin together, resurrecting the language and providing a site for universal progress of the arts and sciences. Maupertuis, a firm believer in progress and enlightenment, seems to assume that if he merely proposed such projects to the princes of his time they would fund them.

In the following section of his *Letter on the Progress of the Sciences*, Maupertuis proposes performing medical and scientific experiments on criminals. While individual rehabilitation or mere discipline have justified punishment in the past, an enlightened society could entertain other utilities. As the real aim of punishment is the Good of Society, why not fulfill that mission more completely? With this justification, surgeries which would otherwise be impossible could well be attempted. Who could oppose the future decrease of suffering for all those innocents afflicted with these maladies? The criminal would not only be contributing to society and progress but would be rewarded by having his sentence annulled. Of course, pain should be reduced to a minimum. These experiments should be performed first on corpses and then on those animals most similar to man. Only after these preliminary alternatives were explored should they move on to the criminals themselves.

Maupertuis suggests beginning with diseases which don't cure themselves naturally and for which the art of medicine has failed to produce remedies. He sneers at those who protest that their

157

medical art is already nearly sufficient and proceeding on the right path. Not so, says our functionary and hero of curiosity. He lauds those who first penetrated the body for kidney stones, drilled holes in the skull, pierced the eyeball. Even more audacious frontiers lie ahead. Progress might well be made on the perplexing question of the relations of the soul and the body, if, instead of engaging in idle metaphysical speculation, one looked for the links by opening up the skull of a living being. While this might seem cruel, the life of one man compared to the species is nothing, and if that life was merely a criminal it was less than nothing. Why not do these things? They benefit humanity and, after all, one leaves to those suffering people up to the end the most precious of commodities, Hope.

Maupertuis calls for more medical specialization, for a more detailed description of nature. More audacious yet, the Prince could provide the material for a kind of natural laboratory. Here naturalists could test such assumptions as the lack of sexual attraction between species. And if they found it to be in fact nature's general rule, perhaps through "education, habit, and need," natural repugnance could itself be modified. Perhaps superior, more useful, species might arise in this manner. Maupertuis asks the Sovereign to promote new kinds of animal curiosities through "intentional, methodical, artful breeding, by means of artificial unions. Curiosity is no longer only the interest in discoverable *curiosa*; it generates them itself." [12]

Blumenberg underlines the fundamental modernity in Maupertuis's proposals. "The curiosity that is no longer in revolt against a reservation—unless it is against the reservation constituted by human indolence vis-à-vis what has not been investigated, or against princely reluctance to finance the necessary large-scale organized attack on what are now becoming the public tasks of theory—this curiosity cannot produce from itself any criterion for its restriction."[13] This point is confirmed by the short list of experiments Maupertuis concludes should *not* be done: further explorations on the philosopher's stone, the squaring of the circle, the problem of perpetual motion. Curiosity's modern norms are futility and utility.

LIFE EXPERIMENTS

Claude Bernard (1813–1877) is generally credited with being the founder of the experimental method in medicine.[14] His explicit goal was to dominate "living nature to conquer it for man's gain." Bernard's active, even aggressive, attitude toward medicine is the opposite of the older Hippocratic approach which sought to facilitate nature's healing qualities. Although Bernard argued that each experiment the physiologist performs should benefit patients, so too, each therapeutic intervention should proceed from and return to advancing a scientific foundation for medical art. Bernard is perfectly consistent in his affirmation that the doctor has the ethical obligation and hence the right to experiment on a living subject as long as the experiment has a chance of "saving his life, curing him or bringing him a personal advantage." For Claude Bernard, in the words of Georges Canguilhem, "To take care is to perform an experiment" (*Soigner, c'est faire une experience*).[15] The best place to learn about how living systems work is *in vivo*.

Claire Ambroselli, in a book on the history of medical ethics, argues that Claude Bernard's conception of experimental medicine—the space between pastoral care and laboratory science—is the place where the distinctly modern tension between the claims of scientific medicine and those of the individual patient come into their sometimes complementary, sometimes antagonistic, but not easily dissolvable relationship. Bernard agrees that the patient's health and rights must be paramount. However, the rights of science, and consequently those of humanity, are equally present in each medical intervention. While this particular patient may not benefit, the knowledge produced will benefit others. Bernard does not flinch from advocating a wide scope, even a mandate, for medical experimentation, or experimentation in the name of medicine. He suggests, for example, experiments on the tissues of those just executed; the physiologist, scalpel poised, waits at the foot of the gallows. He finds it perfectly consistent to conduct research on those just about to die. Carrying his own logic to its conclusions, he advocates the right of the experimenters to

159

experiment on themselves. "Christian morality only forbids one thing, doing wrong (*c'est de faire du mal a son prochain*). Consequently only those experiments on humans which *only* do harm are forbidden, those which are innocuous are permitted and those which could help are prescribed."[16] Bernard knew that his practice could well offend the public. But the physiologist is not an ordinary citizen, he is a scientist absorbed by the pursuit of scientific ideas, "He no longer hears the animals' cries, nor sees the blood which flows, only his idea. The only limits on his action are his own conscience and the opinion of his scientific peers."

Nietzsche's awesome diagnosis of science and modernity, written in 1886, near the end of his productive life, is a good companion for those involved in making a Third Culture. The section on "Mortal Souls" in *The Dawn*, reads: "So far as the promotion of knowledge is concerned, mankind's most useful achievement is perhaps the abandonment of its belief in the immortal soul. Now mankind can wait, now it no longer needs to rush precipitately forward or gulp down ideas only half-tasted, as it formerly had to do. For in the past the salvation of 'eternal soul' depended on a knowledge acquired during a brief lifetime, men had to *come to a decision*, overnight—'knowledge'—possessed a frightful importance. We have reconquered our courage for error, for experimentation, for accepting provisionally—none of it is so very important! And it is for precisely this reason that individuals and generations can now fix their eyes on tasks of a vastness that would to earlier ages have seemed madness and a trifling with Heaven and Hell. We may experiment with ourselves! Yes, mankind now has a right to do that! The greatest sacrifices have not yet been offered to knowledge."[17]

Notes

1. Thanks for helpful comments to Tom White, Frank Rothschild, Troy Duster, Guy Micco, James Faubion, Camille Limoges. This text has been modified more than the others in this volume: it has been trimmed and paragraphs rearranged as a means of providing a lead-in to the concluding essay.

2. C. P. Snow, *Two Cultures: And A Second Look* (Cambridge, U.K.: Cambridge University Press, 1964), p. 9.

3. Ibid., p. 7.

4. Ibid., p. 10.

5. Ibid., pp. 13–14.

6. Ibid., p. 74.

7. Ibid., pp. 76–77.

8. Hans Blumenberg, *The Legitimacy of the Modern Age* (Cambridge, Mass.: MIT Press, 1983; orig. 1966).

9. Ibid., p. 230.

10. Michel Foucault, excavating a different part of the site of Western rationality with very different tools, nonetheless uncovers similar archaeological strata. In his work on the genealogy of the subject—hence of ethics—Foucault outlined the shifting constellations of truth, virtue, and power among the Ancients and the early Christians. Although he did not live to elaborate on it, Foucault indicated a dramatic rupture in this complex tradition when Descartes, in effect, argued that "To accede to truth, it suffices that I be any subject which can see what is evident. . . . Thus I can be immoral and know the truth. I believe that this is an idea which, more or less explicitly, was rejected by all previous cultures. Before Descartes, one could not be impure, immoral, and know the truth. With Descartes, direct evidence is enough." Foucault hypothetizes that this splitting asunder of the ethical subject and knowledge was one of the fundamental preconditions for the technoscientific takeoff of the West.

11. Maupertuis, *Lettre sur le progrès des sciences* (Paris: Collection Palimpseste, Aubier Montaigne, 1980), p. 148. My translation.

12. Ibid., p. 412.

13. Ibid., p. 411.

14. Georges Canguilhem, *Études d'histoire et de philosophie des sciences* (Paris: Vrin, 1983), p. 154.

15. Ibid., p. 389.

16. Ambroselli, *L'Ethique Médicale* (Paris: Presses Universitaires de France, 1988), p. 23.

17. Frederic Nietzsche, *Daybreak: Thoughts on the Prejudices of Morality*, trans. R. J. Hollingdale (Cambridge, U.K.: Cambridge University Press, 1982; Orig. 1886), p. 204.

CHAPTER 9

American Moderns:
On Sciences and Scientists

> We shall set to work and meet the "demands of the
> day," in human relations as well as in our vocation.
> This, however is plain and simple, if each finds
> and obeys the demon who holds the fibers of
> his very life.
> *(Max Weber, "Science as a Vocation")*

HAVING just finished writing the book *Making PCR: A Story of Biotechnology*, I thought it was a good time to reflect on the process
and the stakes of the experience, to return to some of the original
questions I had wrestled with in choosing and defining the research.[1] PCR stands for the polymerase chain reaction, a technology that provides the means to make genetic scarcity into genetic
abundance through exponential amplification of specific sequences of DNA. The story is about the emergent biotech milieu in
which it took shape—the mid-1980s at Cetus Corporation in the
San Francisco Bay Area.

I intended to co-author the book with my main informant, Tom
White, a biochemist, formerly a vice-president of research at
Cetus, currently a vice-president of research and development at
Roche Molecular Systems, a subsidiary of the Swiss multinational
company Hoffmann–La Roche, which bought all the rights to PCR
from Cetus in 1991 for over $300 million. Because ultimately I
wrote the book myself, strictly speaking the experiment in collaboration across the "two cultures" failed to attain its original objective. I do *not* conclude from this fact that the collaboration was a
failure. As the book manuscript neared its completion, I re-posed
a question to Tom that I had previously put to him on several
occasions. "Why had he wanted to work with me?" Typical of his

mode of operation, he provided a written reply, as it would enable him to formulate his thoughts more accurately. White's response does provide reasons why our joint project stalled, but more interestingly it provides insight about how it had been sustained. Tacitly, it also highlights the course of interactions between two Americans, both resolutely modern—but more of that at the end.

As I learned more about how collaborative research operated in the biosciences, I began to realize that there are many ways to shape a project, and, more subtly, diverse ways to receive credit. As the story of how PCR was conceived, invented, coddled, and pushed into becoming a workable technology demonstrates, White was an expert in managing, facilitating, and contributing to the work of others in both direct and indirect manners. In this light, then, let me re-pose the question: What can be learned from this ethnographic experience about the "two cultures," or, more accurately—as the word "culture" is overly general and rather worn out—about two practices?

I have divided White's response into three parts. Each begins with a section of his response and is followed by my commentary. They are entitled "Ethical Substance," "Mode of Subjectivation," "Telos." The divisions parallel in a loose fashion those employed by Michel Foucault in his last writings on ethics and the "technologies of the self." Readers familiar with Foucault will realize that a fourth category, "ethical work," is subsumed under "mode of subjectivation." The essay's fourth section uses Max Weber's 1917 address to students, "Science as a Vocation," as a device to connect these fieldwork reflections to a larger problematization.

ETHICAL SUBSTANCE: EFFICIENCY, CURIOSITY

TOM WHITE: My original contact with Paul Rabinow was via Vince Sarich, who had been a collaborator of Allan Wilson's at U.C. Berkeley while I was a graduate student there in the early 1970s. Sarich explained that Rabinow was interested in learning more about biotechnology and genetic engineering with respect to its current and future cultural implications. Our first meeting occurred in early 1990, about a year after I had left Cetus Corporation to work for Hoffmann–La Roche, where I managed their joint program with Cetus to develop diagnostic applications of a powerful new technology: the polymerase chain reaction. My initial interactions with Paul concentrated mainly on the state of the Human Genome Project and its effect on human identity and forensic analyses. There was also some discussion of the gap in time between genetic diagnosis and the development of new therapies. I also unexpectedly became involved in reviewing Sarich's lecture notes for his Anthro 1 course, where he drew parallels between evolutionary models and contemporary behavior and social policies. During this time, I gained trust in Rabinow by reading one of his books and several articles that grew out of our discussions. He was open to criticism and not intrusive as an observer of seminars and lab meetings.

Over several years, projects that I was involved with provided a rich source of material for Paul's study of scientific cultural practices: the issues and testimony from the scientific community on the novelty of the conception of PCR during Du Pont's challenge of Cetus's patents, writing articles for the AAAS on issues surrounding gene patents, using PCR to test (at the request of NIH's Office of Research Integrity) for the presence of HIV sequences in archival samples from the Gallo and Montagnier labs from the beginning of the AIDS epidemic (and to characterize them), and writing letters requested by the nomination committees for the Japan and Nobel prizes. In turn, I became engaged in some of Paul's projects: the Rice University series, a conference at MIT, and his research at the CEPH. These I found very stimulating both from the subjects being discussed as well as the range of people, interests and perspectives that were so very different from those of my colleagues in biology and medicine.

The "Sarich Affair"

Tom White had known Vincent Sarich, a professor of physical anthropology at Berkeley, from 1971 to 1975, while both were working in the lab of Allan Wilson. During the 1960s and 1970s, Sarich had collaborated with Wilson on breakthrough work on "molecular clocks." They developed new methods of analyzing molecular data, of calculating the divergence times of species such as humans, chimpanzees, and gorillas. Their work fundamentally challenged the prevailing wisdom that the divergence among the great apes was ancient, and provided empirical support for the theory that most mutations are selectively neutral. They were among the first to provide data that changes in the regulation of genes, rather than the steady accumulation of simple mutations, was the cause of major changes in morphology. During the 1980s, Sarich abandoned his scientific research and began to assemble "a worldview," or "philosophy." Sarich labored mightily to combine a variant of libertarianism with an encompassing evolutionary framework. In a fashion typical of autodidacts, Sarich was prepared to explain almost everything. As a venue for his opinions, he began regularly teaching the large (about one thousand student) "Introduction to Physical Anthropology" course at Berkeley—a course usually devoted to primate evolution—and infusing it with his views of society and life.

While over the years there had been some controversy about some of his assertions, especially on intelligence differences between racial groups, these remained isolated incidents. In 1991 Sarich's class was disrupted by students, some in the class and some not, charging him with being racist, sexist, and homophobic. The students objected to Sarich's claims that more hairdressers were homosexual than heterosexual, that there were demonstrable and significant genetic differences in intelligence between groups and genders. Sarich, true to his libertarian principles, always simultaneously maintained that his generalizations never applied to individuals. A public controversy erupted over freedom of speech, the limits of teaching, and the substance of Sarich's claims.

Within the anthropology department, colleagues cast the debate as exclusively a matter of free speech—did one have the absolute right to teach anything in any manner one pleased? The overwhelming response was "yes." Posing the question in this way seemed to me to be overly abstract, formalistic, and juridical. I also knew that once the debate was cast in those terms, it would turn in circles. When I asked if there would be any reason that I should not be allowed to teach a course in molecular biology—I knew the basics just as Sarich knew the basics of philosophy although neither or us had formal training or credentials in the area—the response was an impatient, and barely tolerant, silence.

Among the physical anthropologists at Berkeley, Sarich was the only one who would engage in any public discussions on the substantive scientific claims. The others defended the principle of absolute free speech, defended their turf through appeals to tradition, and went to the local press with inflammatory and fictitious charges of censorship. As a group, they were riven with ferocious rivalries, barely on speaking terms, and were generally all too ready to criticize each other pitilessly, but under these circumstances they closed ranks. The affair *could* have been the occasion to debate what the new configuration of biological and cultural sciences would look like; however, at Berkeley, it didn't turn out that way.

I had undertaken the ethnographic research at a biotech company in part as a kind of political gesture. As older issues of racial inequality were resurfacing in new guises, it seemed important to understand how much the advances in molecular biology could legitimately contribute to these debates. Further, our department (among others) was engaged in a pitched battle over the future construction of the field of anthropology: were there any *intellectual* reasons to believe that the emergent biological and cultural sciences should be in the same department? Berkeley had been the home to the last major synthesis of cultural and physical anthropology. Sherwood Washburn's work on tool making and evolution, for example, was an inspiration and fit snugly with the cutting-edge cultural anthropology of Clifford Geertz, whose article "The Impact of the Concept of Culture on the Concept of Man" announced what seemed to be a new holistic anthropology but proved instead to be the setting sun of such interdisciplinarity. The growing importance of molecular biology, feminism, textual approaches, poststructuralism, and the like opened a new period from which no plausible and sustained interconnections, to say nothing of synthesis, has yet been forged.

Partially for my education and partially as a direct preparation for a panel discussion that we organized around the controversy, I purchased two copies of Sarich's lecture notes for Anthro 1 from a local note-taking service, "Black Lightning." White methodically worked through them, indicating the points he found scientifically questionable, as did I. We might well have been laboring under Max Weber's injunction, laid down in 1911, "What we hope for from racial biologists, . . . is exact evidence of well-defined connections in individual cases, and so of the decisive importance of completely specific hereditary qualities for particular concrete social phenomena. That, gentlemen, does not exist as yet."[2] Except that I hoped for nothing from racial biologists. Regardless, eighty years later, Weber's challenge and conclusion remain pertinent.

During the evening forum on Sarich's work (with several hundred people present) a good deal of political rhetoric was displayed. Afterwards, White and I agreed that the forum and its antecedents were more about the uses and abuses of authority than the specific claims of purported relationships or lack of relationships between genetics and behavior. Dispositionally, we were inclined to share Max Weber's admonition: "Ladies and gentlemen, in the field of science only he who is devoted *solely* to the work at hand has 'personality.' "[3] A cool, decibel-monitored, focus on "the facts" was for White what it meant to "act like a scientist." However, it seems fair to say that my performance at the forum was far less effective at raising issues of broad import and moving the audience to "take a stance" than several of the other panelists. To that extent both White and I were distancing ourselves from overt political action. Though our dispositions and affective temperaments converged, our goals remained unspecified. A degree of mutual trust and acknowledgment of the other's skills and capacities was beginning to take shape between us.

Curiosity

Arising in part out of the forum, White and I thematized an interest in the question of limits (of teaching, of authority, of arenas of investigation, of constraints on inquiry from ideology, of institutional, business or legal constraints). We shared a sense that there was something important at stake in these and related events and developments. One of the things we found missing from the imbroglio was a sense of emergence, of the new knowledges and powers at play, that there might be a new set of problems emerging, ones that would pose different demands. This shared sense led, among other things, to an exchange about "curiosity."

PR: What role does curiosity play in science?
TW: To me curiosity is an extremely powerful motivating factor. You know, food, sex, and shelter and stuff like that. Some of the things we are doing here we don't really know where they lead, you could call it instinct or gut level, but we don't know. Henry Erlich [a senior scientist at Cetus] will justify his work on diabetes [as having commercial potential], and that's the right thing to do, but he just wants to know about how the whole thing works. He doesn't give a damn about whatever else is involved in it. That's why David Gelfand [another senior scientist] has boundless curiosity which takes over what he does.

PR: What are the limits to curiosity?
TW: Boredom. I've seen curiosity end for some scientists. When it does end it is a totally recognizable element in them. They no longer have the curiosity. They go home at five o'clock. Or they say, "Well, if you want me to write up the paper, I am going to have to take some time off from work," rather than write it at night or on the weekend like everyone else does. Or when some peculiar result is presented at meetings, they yawn and aren't interested. It is the strangest thing. It's like death in a scientist. They can be productive in a certain sense, but the ability to solve new problems isn't there.

PR: So, curiosity can die and become routine and boredom. But what about the other side: can you have too much curiosity?
TW: Yes, some people are so curious that they never complete anything. One idea after another idea but all at a level that's not very

deep so you can't determine the complexity. What's workable or not. The science fiction mode sets the limits of curiosity when humans mate with apes and meddle with God's work kind of thing. The limits for scientists are that scientists' visions are limited socially. Many of them never even conceive some issues, for example, how the family is defined. These people are thinking about how to detect hemoglobin S from hemoglobin A; they don't think how this will affect families.

PR: Is curiosity a good thing?
TW: It's getting the answer to your curiosity. The mouse pushing on the button to get more cocaine. There is something intensely gratifying about satisfying your curiosity. Scientists just want to know the answer to something. That's why David Gelfand is in the lab every Sunday; he just wants to know how the thing works. Those who are motivated by curiosity have the problem of stopping. They ruin social occasions.

PR: I've written a paper called "The Curious Patient," which was inspired by Hans Blumenberg's chapter on curiosity in *The Legitimacy of the Modern Age*. Blumenberg talks about curiosity as one of the great motive forces of the Enlightenment. He shows how curiosity is something that has been consistently under attack by Christianity and other authority structures. But modernity faces the question of what are the limits to curiosity? There were the German medical and scientific experiments and so many others in the United States and elsewhere which obviously crossed the line of acceptable research or clinical practice. Perhaps there are no self-limiting principles within science itself to tell you not to do a particular experiment? Since curiosity and modernity combine to drive endlessly toward producing something new, perhaps the combination of newness and curiosity's boundlessness is the problem? Perhaps these German scientists who worked on living patients were horrible human beings, but we now know that they were not all horrible scientists. This disjunction is troubling. The core of the distinguished German medical establishment went along with the Nazis. Curiosity has its thresholds. Perhaps it is

169

ethics or religion or politics or aesthetics (as Nietzsche thought) which limits what one can and cannot do—not science.

TW: That boundary where curiosity goes over into something unethical could also be an element in some aspects of scientific problems. They are always ascribed to power and priority issues, but there is an element of curiosity affecting the ability to interpret your data. Sometimes, people see the results they want to see. Others falsify their experiments, others simply ignore the data that doesn't fit.

Curiosity does get to a point where judgment is required. One boundary to examine is, when does curiosity reach a limit? How would that decision be made? Since there isn't an independent referee, what sort of process does one go through to arrive at a stopping point? What would you draw on to make that decision? Not a simple question: what to do to access resources? That what you do might be unethical? Or socially advisable?

Tom was quite right that molecular biology has no principle internal to its field of practice by which to pose the question of limits. For the human sciences, it *is* possible to practice them in such a fashion that the question of limits, as well as the reflexive thematization of that concern, constitutes a central dimension of the project itself. Reflexivity, however, like rationality, means many different things. Just as one could formulate a practice that foregrounds political awareness and action, so, too, one could engage in a practice that attempted to make "ethical" action calculable and rationalized. Reflexivity could mean methodologically searching for a normative scale that could be cast in operationalizable terms; work in many areas of bioethics is involved in constituting such a practice. Another direction, the one I pursued, cast reflexivity as an experiential and experimental "problem," one not amenable to the kind of bureaucratic requirements many bioethicists faced, one not directly "useful." This stance entails being curious about scientific curiosity and curious about one's own curiosity. It leads one to thematize the form of life that surrounds, sustains, and undermines curiosity. Thus, even when claims are made to have discovered "the curiosity gene," the question of what kind of society has posed such questions to itself, why it has sought to produce this type of knowledge, will remain open. So, too, the question will remain of how best to situate oneself in relation to that knowledge, that society, and those goals.

Mode of Objectivity: Ethical Work

Tom White: [a]rticles were beginning to appear in the popular scientific literature about PCR's "uncommon" origin [by Kary Mullis, its "inventor"]. These were counterbalanced or paralleled by other accounts from Cetus's management and public relations office. From my perspective, as the former VP of Research at Cetus, none of the accounts gave an accurate picture of the circumstances and milieu that had led to PCR. In fact, they reinforced certain stereotypes about scientists (the unappreciated genius working alone) and science in industry (closed, unimaginative, plodding) that bore no relation at all to the way science was done in one of the first biotechnology companies.

I had made a preliminary effort to write my observations about the history of PCR, but also felt I was too close to the events to portray them objectively. What was needed was someone with a different background than those involved directly, i.e., not a typical memoir from a retired authority figure, nor a journalistic account that emphasized gossip or rivalries. An anthropologist seemed about right to me. Furthermore, an anthropologist would be able to place current scientific practice into a broader framework of other cultural practices and theory, so that whatever was truly unique about the PCR experience, if anything, would be visible.

Consistently unharried amidst a multitude of responsibilities, White is not casual. He is simultaneously goal-oriented and systematically flexible in finding appropriate means to attain his objectives. Emblematic of this stance to me was a complex multidimensional chart White had on his office wall, outlining the steps necessary (over the course of several years) to coordinate work toward commercializing a set of diagnostic tests. The chart had replaced an equally large cross-cultural "timeline" of world history. The charts functioned as a map in the sense of portraying objectives and functional conjuncture points; White never took them as rigid guidelines for action, nor as "filled-in." He prides himself on maintaining close contact with those directly involved in working out technical details, since experience shows him that these are the people who have the most precise knowledge of difficulties and solutions. White coordinates and manages, he is responsible for the larger picture. As he indicates, White was dispositionally prepared for someone to propose a project on the invention of PCR, even if he was not actively searching for such a person. My proposal fit a space on some imaginary chart. That is one reason White responded so rapidly to my overtures. He was clearer than I about the project, at least initially and in the sense outlined above. But again, he left the strategy and details of working it out to me, almost never initiating research directions but constantly being available for responses and help.

White has formulated a set of evaluative benchmarks in order to judge the performance and character of scientists and their work. Upon meeting me, White began evaluating my person and character (credentials, strengths, and weaknesses, personality in terms of potential collaboration, idiosyncrasies, etc.), just as he would with anyone with whom he had or might have a working relationship. After a series of formally arranged interviews about general issues in molecular biology and genetics (the Human Genome Project, etc.), he extended his observations to my preliminary ethnographic work at Roche Diagnostic Research, the complex of labs whose research he directed. I was under scrutiny at the lab meetings I attended (highly technical discussions about diagnostic tests in a variety of stages of development) as well as in my follow-up discussions with individual scientists. He discreetly—and appropriately—monitored both. He and the other scientists and technicians concurred that I was learning enough molecular biology to follow the discussions, and that I was acting responsibly (not pursuing confidential materials on probe design, sharing reactions of one scientist with others, etc.). White strongly demurred when I remarked that the "techs" were so responsive to my questions mainly because of my connection to him; he was adamant that although his authorization was necessary for me to be in the labs at all, it was not sufficient. Each of his colleagues and technicians was exercising his or her own autonomous judgment. They knew his management style of monitored independence, maximized flow of information, and critical evaluation of people and procedures up and down the hierarchy. White strongly believed that maximizing autonomy (within a project-oriented structure) produced better results; it was more efficient, it was better for human relations, it maximized responsibility at each level. Modern to the hilt. I showed that I was willing and able to conform behaviorally to this normative structure, and White was wagering that he was correctly evaluating my character as well.

White had three important objectives: he wanted to arrive at an *accurate* picture of the circumstances and the milieu of contemporary biotechnology from which a very important invention had emerged; he represented himself as being too close to the events and the actors to be in a position to portray them *objectively*; in his view, an anthropologist had the right distance and the right perspective to make the event's uniqueness *visible*. White is fully aware that an *accurate, objective,* and *visible* account could be put to many different purposes. In his statement he does not make reference to the fact that the meaning of each of these terms is highly contested in the human sciences. Consequently, White's framing of the project is simultaneously, and characteristically, transparent and opaque. It is transparent insofar as it is impelled by a desire to have a literally correct and appropriately coherent account of a major scientific and technological breakthrough. White's project is opaque to me in its unadorned, confident choice of "an anthropologist" to produce such an account. White had been in the Peace Corps in Africa during the 1960s and had learned a good deal (partially from reading anthropological accounts but mainly through his experiences) about the language and culture of the Loma people in Liberia (he was especially intrigued by the

Loma's different use of parabolic language: representations of dimensional space, on a system of counting). He has even published an ethnohistory by a Loma elder.

White was not naive about anthropology; he knew that anthropology was embroiled in major disputes about the status of representations, textuality, and power. His familiarity with this state of affairs extended to *Writing Culture*. Shortly before I began working with him, his wife, Leslie Scalapino, a well-known poet and publisher of an avant-guard press, O Books, had been engaged in a series of polemic skirmishes with the editor of *Socialist Review* that paralleled some of the debates within anthropology that surrounded *Writing Culture*. I invited Scalapino to express her views on these debates. Although I was interested in her views per se, I was also curious about the discussions she and Tom had about the prospects of his working with me.

LS: There were many things I found interesting about your article ["Representations are Social Facts"]. For example, when you are talking about Fredric Jameson's analysis of postmodern culture, it is interesting to me that Jameson, in what has now become a rather famous essay, attacked one of the language poets, Bob Perelman. It's interesting to me because much of what's being done in poetry now is very similar to the kinds of questions you're raising in your article. Much current writing has to do with analyzing perception itself, one's own subjectivity, as the placement of the writer or the viewer vis à vis what's being written. Jameson's argument has been regarded by many people in the literary community as an example of a very conservative, yet Marxist, argument in which he criticized contemporary poetics as dislocated in the direction of being merely fragmentary. Meaning that which is modern is seen as chaotic.

The language group of writers, who are themselves of a Marxist orientation, are proponents of form scrutinizing itself. Jameson is regarded in his essay as demanding a very hierarchical and centralized view of writing where there would be no room for any kind of varied perspective or examination of perspective itself.

174

Tom told me that you have read an exchange between the language poet, Ron Silliman, and myself whose subject was feminism, gays, and so-called minority perspective as incompatible with avant-garde or experimental work. In this exchange, I was answering an essay by Ron that was published in the *Socialist Review* about six poets, including myself. Actually, our exchange was much larger than what you saw, having occurred over a period of about a year. It was impossible to get any answer of mine to his essay to be published in the *Socialist Review*. They described my initial reply as being too poetic and rejected it on the basis that it was not political discourse. To which I objected that they could not, should not, determine the form and thus the nature of political discourse. Before our exchange could be published later in another journal, the male editor wanted us to rewrite it in a more orderly format. He disagreed with Ron's argument and considered my tone to be hostile. We did not revamp our exchange but shortened it. My original tone in our correspondence was stronger, but this gradually changed. Ironically, the editor was criticizing the later, softer tone.

While the culture wars rage in the human sciences ("incommensurability," "post-identity," "post-narrativity," and the like), White and his fellow scientists—several of whom read parts of each of the multiple drafts of *Making PCR*—never once raised epistemo logical objections to my approach. They corrected details, they debated the applicability of terms like "technocrat," they insisted on "accuracy" but refrained from objecting to my use of form and interpretation. "It's your book," was the common refrain. This reserve is entirely uncharacteristic of the practice of molecular biologists (or other scientists) among themselves where strong criticism is the norm.

This turn of events remains perplexing to me. Does it mean that these molecular biologists are moderns, i.e., nonhegemonic, pluralistic, even perspectival, about things social? The answer, at least partially, is "Yes." White and his colleagues *are* moderns, and several of the senior scientists had an active interest in writings about science. Several others aside from White have spouses in the art world. Henry Erlich, whose wife runs the ODC San Francisco dance company, is a keen fan of the novels of Richard Powers such as *The Goldbug Variations* or *Galatea 2.2*. They are also Americans; they exhibit none of the pathos or tragedy that for others has accompanied the "diversity of value spheres." Richard Rorty would approve of their nonplussed attitude.

The flexibility about textual form and tolerance for multiple interpretation when it comes to society must be juxtaposed to the standardization of scientific writing and interpretation to which all good scientists adhere. As the ethnography shows, these molecular biologists would not assent to the following assertion from Pierre Bourdieu: "I hold that, all the scholastic discussions about the distinctiveness of the human sciences not withstanding, the human sciences are subject to the same rules that apply to all sciences.[. . .] I am struck, when I speak with my friends who are chemists, physicians, or neurobiologists, by the similarities between their practice and that of a sociologist. The typical day of a sociologist, with its experimental groping, statistical analysis, reading of scholarly papers, and discussion with colleagues, looks very much like that of an ordinary scientist to me."[4] The obligatory flat joke that greeted me in labs in France and the U.S. was always "now we will be put under the microscope" or "he's here to treat us like guinea pigs." The lines came from scientists who used neither microscopes (computers and PCR machines) nor employed guinea pigs (yeast and viruses). These jokes disappeared immediately once our work was underway; they reveal an initial anxiety about being objectified, nothing more. Ethnographically and experientially, the analogy is a bad one and its use as a metaphor is even worse.

Juxtaposing two quotes, one from Pierre Bourdieu and the other from Kary Mullis, both from methods sections of larger works, one from sociology and one from molecular biology, rhetorically underscores the point. First, Bourdieu: "In order to escape the *realism of the structure*, which hypostatizes systems of ob-

jective relations by converting them into totalities already constituted outside of individual history and group history, it is necessary to pass from the *opus operatum* to the *modus operandi*, from
statistical regularity or algebraic structure to the principle of the
production of this observed order, and to construct the theory of
practice or, more precisely, the theory of the mode of generation
of practices, which is the precondition for establishing an experimental science of the *dialectic of the internalization of externality and
the externalization of internality*, or more simply, of incorporation
and objectification."[5] Although I more or less understand what
Bourdieu means, I have not met a single biologist who does and,
for that matter, very few anthropologists who do. Second, in contrast, Kary Mullis, the inventor of the polymerase chain reaction,
discusses his "methods" in the following terms: "Oligonucleotides
were synthesized using an automated DNA synthesis machine (Bio-
search Inc., San Rafael, California) using phosphoroamidite
chemistry. Synthesis and purification were performed according
to the directions provided by the manufacturer."[6] Mullis's account
is transparent to those working in his field and appropriately
opaque to those who don't practice it.

Bourdieu works in a pluralistic scientific milieu and he regrets
it. Mullis, on the other hand, lives in a milieu that has stabilized
experimental practices and textual genres reporting those practices. When Mullis conceived of the polymerase reaction, he was
convinced that he had thought of a revolutionary invention; he
was slow, however, to produce either experimental proof or to
write up his experimental results. White and others put tremen-
dous pressure on him to do both.

In 1985, at the end of two years of intense work by two teams at
Cetus Corporation attempting to make the polymerase chain reaction work consistently and efficiently, the scientists finally were
getting results that satisfied them. They decided to publish a paper
announcing the new method. Following a commonly employed
procedure, they re-ran a set of experiments, so that they would
have "elegant" results for the paper. I did something similiar in the
last draft of the book. However, I had a choice of quite disparate

177

ways of bringing the project to completion, including emphasizing the disparities and blockages along the way or underplaying them. It seems self-evident that the practices of the Cetus scientists and my own differed. The relation of textual form to experimental practice has been stabilized in the biological sciences in a fashion that the human sciences have never achieved.

Even assuming that one could find an equivalent of the laboratory practices of molecular biology among anthropologists and sociologists, the relationship of the experimental situation to the texts that report on that setting present stark differences. There is a great diversity of experimental practice in the human sciences and a great diversity of textual practice as well. Although the coming triumph of a physical science model in the human sciences has been announced for several centuries—what I have called the "cargo cult view" of science—it has never happened. Empirically the only way it could, would be through political means in which all opposition would be eliminated (defunded, detenured, etc.).

In his remarkable paper entitled "Why Is There No Hermeneutics of the Natural Sciences?" the Hungarian philosopher Gyorgy Markus synthesizes current research in the history, philosophy, and sociology of science. Markus underlines the central dividing point: "Natural scientific activities involve in our culture not only argumentative-discursive but also experimental-manipulative practices. Therefore new knowledge is fixed and accumulated in this field not merely in the form of textual objectivations, but also through incorporation into those lab activities which have the character of craft skills and can only be learned through example and controlled performances in the relevant situations. All the observation terms are linked to that action arena. As a result, an adequate understanding of natural scientific texts cannot be learned/acquired in an intercourse with these texts alone. The craft skill is shared only by the group of specialists." Markus is fully aware that textual production in the human sciences (itself quite diverse) is linked to other practices as well. His point is that these arts and practices differ. The differences are anything but scholastic. Erasing them through metaphor—Bourdieu's "experimental gropings"—is ethnographically unconvincing.

Employing categories from "reader-response" theory, Markus asks, who is the implied subject in natural scientific texts? He analyzes the textual devices that contribute to constructing an impersonal subject as the author of the scientific article. Chief among these devices is the imperative to remove all textual traces of the vagaries, accidents, special circumstances, unusual skills, and fortune involved in a piece of work. Markus writes, "The "inscribed author" of the natural scientific texts appears as an anonymous performer of methodologically certified, strictly regulated activities and a detached observer of the results—without any further personal identifying remarks beyond possession of the required professional competence. [. . .] It is essential that the 'scientific anyman' could have been the author of the paper."[7] The same textual criteria apply to the audience; these devices make possible the complete interchangeability of the author and the audience. It follows that only those who share the experimental practices (often restricted to a subspecialty) are fully capable of understanding and evaluating such texts. Hence, their strength and their limitation are one and the same thing.

Markus concludes that there is no hermeneutics of the natural sciences because there is no need for one. Scientific writing "is culturally defined as of no interest or consequence for a non-specialist reader." In fact, growing technical mastery and specialization in the natural sciences yield a progressive narrowing of cultural significance because "the view of nature provided by the sciences is no more a world-view."[8] This 'lack of a world view,' 'this narrowing,' this cultural triumph, is itself a condition for the technical efficacy of modern science. In a strict sense, there is no self-questioning within molecular biology. From time to time, there are debates about the ends to which results could be put, political projects that might be dangerous or beneficial; there are occasional discussions about the composition (gender, race, class) of the social body of scientists, but the normative parameters of the textual and nondiscursive practices of sciences like molecular biology are not a question of philosophic debate among practitioners. The plethora of "worldview" books—with punchy adolescent titles—produced by science journalists and aging scientists underscores the point.

A parallel situation does not exist in the human sciences. No one, above all Pierre Bourdieu himself, has ever mistaken his writings for the social-scientific everyman; their distinction immediately sets them apart. It is true that mimicking the subject and reader positions of the natural sciences is one option available to practitioners of various human sciences. It is, however, only one option among others, one style among others, one rhetoric among others. The utter lack of success in achieving unity in the human sciences (except from time to time under totalitarian political conditions) does not prove that the human sciences will never "come of age," but it does underscore the distinctive historical and sociological uniqueness in the achievement of such textual unity in the natural sciences. Their strength is their weakness, their weakness their strength.

Telos

TOM WHITE: "The motivations for my interest in this collaboration are several: there are a number of disturbing phenomena and trends in contemporary science that parallel society at large; there are widespread stereotypes of scientists in industry that are destructive and counterproductive to improvements in health care; there are preconceived notions about the genomic diversity project that are anti-intellectual, patronizing, and perpetuate delusions about our knowledge of the origin and migratory history of modern peoples; an interest in scientific communication and collaboration per se.

As an example of the first phenomenon, leading international scientific journals have increasingly become the vehicles for tabloid news articles on scientific rivalries, misconduct, patent and credit disputes, etc. The use of anonymous sources, leaked confidential documents, erroneous information, and unchecked claims is the new(s) standard for *Nature* and *Science.* These journals are so influential and reputable in their peer-reviewed articles that credence carries over to their tabloid reports. The editors also occasionally perpetuate the stereotypes of "pure" academic scientists and of industrial scientists only being motivated by money and profit, while conveniently ignoring the corrupting influence of "academic capital", e.g., membership on editorial boards, grant agency peer-review panels, FDA reviewer of a company's application while serving as a paid consultant to its competitor, and other conflicts of interest that are not usually designated as such within the academy. These models lead some influential scientists to exhibit behaviors usually associated with creationists or fundamentalists: claiming the absolute moral high ground, a fondness for conspiracy and catastrophe scenarios, and a complete disregard for facts. The trends are certainly rampant in society at large in the form of a willful blindness to societal problems and a delusionary momentum to find simplistic causes and solutions while claiming to be pragmatic and revolutionary.

So, one of my purposes in helping Paul write the PCR book was to arrive at an account of an extraordinary genetic discovery that could show how to create an environment for future discoveries. Furthermore, this account would counteract other "histories" that, in my view, perpetuate the very conditions and stereotypes that destroy creativity and the process of discovery. This would be done by providing a cultural anthropologist unique access to the scientists, from technicians to department heads to top managers, etc., of a biotechnology company. Perhaps this would also overcome the misplaced conservatism of private institutions about allowing such access and openness if the company, its scientists, and their anthropological collaborator could conduct themselves in a principled, creative, and productive way. After all, how else can society arrive at the best-informed decisions on the ethical, legal, and social issues arising both from new technologies and information and also from the methods of investigating them?

White wants simultaneously to defend the traditional boundaries of modern science as a practice while extending the institutional sites in which such science can be seen to be legitimately prac-

181

ticed. Many scientists I have talked with (both within and without the university and both in Europe and the U.S.) complain that *Nature* and *Science* are illicitly trading on the authority as leading scientific journals. The depth of the resentment is striking. Its source seems to be boundary anxiety; any practicing bioscientist today is keenly aware of the politics of science, especially the funding priorities, competition, and its discontents, and so on. They seem willing to tolerate, while lamenting, the current state of affairs as long as there is a protected inner sanctum of science played by the rules. White and his colleagues defend the biotech industry as a legitimate and competitive alternative to the university or governmental labs. When part of the Nobel Prize in chemistry in 1993 was awarded for the invention of PCR, White saw this event as a major threshold validating the quality of science done outside the university.

For White, an anthropologist might serve as a situated observer but one who could explore the effect of his partiality on the subject matter. "Part of an experimental exploration is not knowing what you may find. My attitude about an anthropologist studying PCR, and my colleagues notion of not 'directing' him, is in some measure a desire to let the anthropologist discover something (a pattern, process or paradigm?) about what happened. It was intended to see if he might produce a new form." In that sense, he hoped that the collaboration could make him more productive. He never blurred the distinction between the technical and the therapeutic; he never asked me to play a "facilitator" or "therapeutic" role. White remained attentive to possible operationalizable aspects arising from my analysis. One thing he wanted to know was "how to create an environment for future discoveries." White was engaged from the start in an experiment in which I was being deployed as much as the other way around. This experiment was one he could manage and monitor but not control. There were risks involved for him in such a strategy; my presence might have occasioned interpersonal trouble in the lab; his corporate superiors might have disapproved of the whole project. Neither happened. In the last stages of the writing, a lawyer at Hoffmann–La Roche was informed that legal advisers had suggested that Roche scientists modify a few of their own quotations (about lawyers) in the book. They told White they were "not in the business of censorship." White never asked for a right of veto of my material, nor was he ever offered one.

Why did he engage in this experiment? Partially his strong desire "to set the record straight," partially his curiosity about what I would produce, no doubt some ego gratification, an affirmation of his own self-image as an unconventional facilitator, resolutely operating in dissonance or at least in a productive tension with his well-heeled surfaces. Mainly, White wanted to practice his science in a certain manner, "to work at the limits of one's ability and curiosity with as few resources and restrictions as possible."[9] He wanted to be working in an environment in which such collaboration would be considered normal. It was a risk worth taking. After all, White and his colleagues were practitioners who spent their lives in environments of calculated risk. It was part of their professional disposition to try things and see what happens. The biotechnology industry occupies a large place in certain sectors of molecular biological research. The fact that as few as one in five grants are being funded by governmental agencies in the U.S. indicates that fundamental changes are taking place in the institutional arrangements for supporting science that emerged after the Second World War. Without money there is no research in these fields, and an increasing percentage of that research is being done in nongovernmental or university settings. White and his colleagues had chosen to work for a biotechnology company where the literal calculation of financial risk was directly on the agenda in a way that it wasn't in a university environment. They were, as it were, professional controlled risk takers operating in a fluid environment structured by availability of funds, technological limitations, legal constraints, and their dispositions.

DEMANDS OF THE DAY: BETWEEN EFFICIENCY AND WORLDVIEW

Max Weber's lecture "Science as a Vocation," delivered in 1917 on the day of the Bolshevik seizure of power and near the end of the First World War, contains the classic statement of the place and problem of science (*Wissenschaft*) in modernity understood as a cultural and economic formation as well as an ethos. Weber's remarks provide a touchstone for testing the vexed, if allusive, question of the status of science and modernity, postmodernity, and amodernity in the light of specific ethnographic research on contemporary biotechnology and its practitioners. More importantly, they put forth a hypothesis about the limits of the sciences and the demands posed by those limits.

Weber identified the gradually accumulating spread of rationalization processes, from calculative rationality to bureaucratization, to the methodical organization of everyday life, as the key diacritic of modernity. The mark of modernity—and here is where *Wissenschaft* enters—is demagification (*Entzauberung*). Demagification means *principled* disenchantment, not the total control or general flattening of life. Such principled disenchantment does indeed open the cultural and ethical possibility of nihilism, or postmodernity, but does not entail it. On this often misunderstood point, Weber could not be clearer: "The increasing intellectualization and rationalization do *not*, therefore indicate an increased and general knowledge of the conditions under which one lives. It means something else, namely, the knowledge or belief that if one but wished one could learn it at any time. This means that the world is disenchanted."[10] In the sphere of meaning, the mark of modernity is fracture and pluralism. The gradual institutionalization of science applied the fracturous blow to older worldviews, not forceably destroying them, only decentering them, relativizing them, placing them in a relational position. Scientific practice created a sphere in which the dark and joyous forces of enchantment and meaning were banished, stilled. Although—the point is often missed—Weber is quite clear, such forces continue to flourish: "Fate, and certainly not science, holds sway over these gods [Aphrodite and Apollo] and their struggles."[11] Many other social and cultural instances give shape to "these gods" beyond fate. Normatively, however, science stands against the principled hegemony of such forces. Modernity is the principle of demagification, not its colonial triumph. Weber follows Nietzsche in signaling plurality of value as modernity's fate, its triumph and dilemma.

This multiplication of cultural possibilities problematizes the place of the knowledge seeker. Science (*Wissenschaft*) only provides the tools for a growing technical mastery of the world, both natural and social. "Natural science gives us an answer to the question of what we must do if we wish to master life technically. It leaves quite aside, or assumes for its purposes, whether we should and do wish to master life technically and whether it ultimately makes sense to do so."[12] Weber had nothing but a haughty contempt for those spokesmen (of all political stripes) who believed that science could and ought to play such a role. "Who," Weber ironized, "aside from certain big children who are indeed found in the natural sciences—still believes that the findings of astronomy, biology, physics, or chemistry could teach us anything about the *meaning* of the world?"[13] Further, who believed science was the path to the Enlightenment goal of happiness, "aside from a few big children in university chairs or editorial offices"?[14] Those who claim today that the Human Genome Project is the "holy grail" fall squarely within the infantile tradition, as do those who take their ant colonies as metaphors or, worse, metonyms of all collectivities. But, so too, do those who see *only* status striving in human existence.

According to Weber, science (*Wissenschaft*) does three things. It "contributes to the technology of controlling life by calculating external objects as well as man's activities. [It] contributes methods of thinking, the tools and training for thought. [It] helps us to gain clarity."[15] The demand of self-clarification places the issue of *Lebensführung*, or life-regulation, at center stage both as an object of study and as an ethical problem. It is precisely these issues that Michel Foucault's analytic of ethics was grappling with as well. Foucault defines the "telos" of ethical activity as "that activity in which one finds the self. An action is not only moral in itself, in its singularity; it is also moral in its circumstantial integration and by virtue of the place it occupies in a pattern of conduct." The key terms are the "circumstantial integration" and the "place it occupies in a pattern of conduct." These terms are uncannily close to and simultaneously far from "technical efficiency" and "worldview."

What is that circumstantial integration? And what is the pattern of conduct? To what extent did I or could I integrate Tom's goals into my pattern of conduct? I had no stakes in or fantasies about improving industry (and was not optimistic about the academy), although the goal of interacting with scientists in "a principled, creative, and productive way," and hence to aid the task of inventing a milieu where we could do so, was at the core of the project. I share Tom's desire to counteract the "stereotypes that destroy creativity and the process of discovery," but not his tenacious optimism about fulfilling that desire. I don't have any programmatic intention of showing "how to create an environment for future discoveries." Ultimately, for me the thorniest part of the quotation is found at the end of Tom's statement: "After all, how else can society arrive at the best-informed decisions on the ethical, legal, and social issues arising both from new technologies and information and also from the methods of investigating them?"

How else? For Tom, this phrase was his basic question, one that underscores how he framed the demands of the day. The phrase made me agitated. My experience has not been that "society" often sought to arrive at the best-informed decisions. Or, more accurately, what funding agencies, federal bureaucracies, or legal instances and parliamentary bodies considered to be "informed" was often completely exotic—and irredeemably alienating. When I applied to the Social, Legal and Ethics division of the Department of Energy's Human Genome Project for a grant to study PCR, I was told PCR was not relevant to the Genome Project, even though admittedly the project would have been basically impossible without it. Social science should study what happened to the discoveries of molecular biology, not the molecular biologists and their practices; Charles Cantor, then director of the Genome Project at Berkeley, told me that PCR "had no social consequences, just like the transistor." When I applied to the National Institutes of Health Human Genome Project to study the different approach to genome mapping being undertaken in France by the CEPH, I was told there were no significant differences in approach (this was before the French beat the Americans in producing the first physical map of the human genome). The official letter of rejection informed me that my working "hypothesis" about studying the production of genetic knowledge in different cultures was poorly formulated because all significant human differences were biological, not cultural. When I asked the anthropologist-ethicist-bureaucrat who was charged with overseeing these evaluations whether he believed all significant differences were biological, he told me their evaluation procedures had been fair. When I asked him if he had fallen off his chair laughing, he didn't respond. With the passage of time, and disregarding the simple asininity involved, I have come to find these responses almost coherent: given their assumptions, how else could an Ethics Bureaucracy operate "to achieve the best-informed decisions"? It is the assumptions—that one needs to show how to proceed from a worldview (theory) to a technical problem (hypothesis) and that bureaucracies should be charged with ethics—that are curious.

Yet, White *had* responded to my overtures by providing me with the opportunity to do research, in part because he thought such research would help him to make informed decisions and to create and sustain an innovative environment. It would make something different happen that he couldn't entirely control. White, after all, is a hyperactive optimist by temperament. He also has a career record of making environments from which discoveries do emerge and new forms of experimentation are possible. In this light, it is worth noting that White had been approached in the early days of the Human Genome Project about heading the Department of Energy program. He did not pursue the opening, deciding instead to stay in industry. Although I am a hyperactive pessimist, I *had* integrated the circumstantial opportunity into my pattern of conduct. The incidental movements that led me to White, to the polymerase chain reaction, to Cetus Corporation, yielded, as far as I can tell, neither technical efficiency nor a worldview. It produced a book. I gained some experience and perhaps a certain clarity from the experiment. Who, aside from some big children in university chairs, government bureaus, and editorial offices, could ask for anything more?

Notes

1. Paul Rabinow, *Making PCR: A Story of Biotechnology* (Chicago: University of Chicago Press, 1996).

2. "Sociology and Biology," in W. G. Runciman, ed., *Weber: Selections in Translation* (Cambridge, U.K.: Cambridge University Press, 1978), p. 390.

3. Max Weber,"Science as a Vocation," in H. Gerth and C. Wright Mills, eds., *From Max Weber* (New York: Oxford University Press, 1946), p. 137.

4. Pierre Bourdieu and Loic Wacquant, *An Introduction to Reflexive Sociology* (Chicago: University of Chicago Press, 1992), p. 185.

5. Pierre Bourdieu, *Outline of a Theory of Practice* (Cambridge, U.K.: Cambridge University Press, 1977), p. 72.

6. Kary B. Mullis and Fred A. Faloona, "Specific Synthesis of DNA in vitro via a Polymerase-Catalyzed Chain Reaction," *Methods in Enzymology* 15 (1987): 339.

7. Gyorgy Markus, "Why Is There No Hermeneutics of the Natural Sciences? Some Preliminary Theses," *Science in Context* 1 (1987): 29.

8. Ibid., p. 29.

9. Tom White, pers. comm., January 10, 1996.

10. Weber, "Science as a Vocation," p. 139.

11. Ibid., p. 149.

12. Ibid., p. 144.

13. Ibid., p. 142.

14. Ibid., p. 143.

15. Ibid., pp. 150–51.

Index

Encountering Development:
The Making and Unmaking of the Third World
by Arturo Escobar

Social Bodies:
Science, Reproduction, and Italian Modernity
by David G. Horn

Revisioning History:
Film and the Construction of a New Past
edited by Robert A. Rosenstone

The History of Everyday Life:
Reconstructing Historical Experiences and Ways of Life
edited by Alf Lüdtke

The Savage Freud and Other Essays on Possible
and Retrievable Selves
by Ashis Nandy

Children and the Politics of Culture
edited by Sharon Stephens

Intimacy and Exclusion:
Religious Politics in Pre-Revolutionary Baden
by Dagmar Herzog

What Was Socialism, and What Comes Next?
by Katherine Verdery

Citizen and Subject:
Contemporary Africa and the Legacy of Late Colonialism
by Mahmood Mamdani

Colonialism and Its Forms of Knowledge: The British in India
by Bernard S. Cohn

Charred Lullabies: Chapters in an Anthropography of Violence
by E. Valentine Daniel

Theft of an Idol:
Text and Context in the Representation of
Collective Violence
by Paul R. Brass

Essays on the Anthropology of Reason
by Paul Rabinow